Church Website Design

A Step By Step Approach

Church Website Design
A Step By Step Approach
Timothy Fish

Church Website Design: A Step By Step Approach

To order additional copies, please contact:
BookSurge, LLC
www.booksurge.com
1-866-308-6235
orders@booksurge.com

While no harm is foreseen and great care has been taken in the preparation of this book, neither the author nor the publisher assume any responsibility for errors or omissions, or for damages resulting from the use of the information contained herein or in any of the sources mentioned. It is impossible for the author to know the situation of every reader, so it is the responsibility of the reader to determine if any of the products and services mentioned in this book will work for the reader's situation.

Table of Contents

Preface:
The Purpose and Audience

The internet continues to grow and it seems like there are more people using it as a primary source of information every year. Some of these people are looking for a church home or for other information and services that churches provide. It is my belief that most churches can better minister to their communities and membership with a website than what they can without one.

While many people are aware of their church's need for a website and many people have a desire for their church to have a website, they may be uncertain about what needs to be done in order to make this possible. Some people have taken efforts to create a church website, but they have found that keeping the site up to date is a chore.

This book is intended for people who are at least considering developing a church website as well as for people who already have a church website and are looking for ways to improve it. It takes a step by step approach that I believe anyone who has the willingness to learn can follow all the way from having no knowledge of how to develop a website to having an attractive, usable and maintainable website that is available for all the world to see.

This book is not intended to be a definitive guide on how to develop websites. There are too many technologies available for that to be possible. Other books and websites cover these individual technologies. This book is intended to be much more practical. By focusing on the specific task of developing a church website, the book makes it possible to develop a functioning website without the need to spend a lot of time sorting through all of the information that is available and deciding which technologies apply and which don't.

Readers who wish to use a different technology and readers who already have a church website will still find useful information within this book. While the code will not function in quite the same way for different technologies, the basic concepts remain the same. The sections that describe how to design the website and many of the other aspects of church website development will still apply. The reader need only adjust his implementation to use the chosen technology.

Pastor's and other church leaders who may not be interested in the technical aspects will still find this book helpful to guide them to an understanding and an appreciation for the work that is required to develop a church website. If you are reading the book for that purpose and intend to let someone else do the technical work required, I suggest skipping Step 5, skimming through Step 6 and Step 7 and skipping Step 8 while you are reading. These steps are the most technical and will be of little use to the reader who is not sitting at a computer ready to type code.

Let the creative juices flow. While the code provided in this book is enough to create a functioning website, your website development effort will be a whole lot more fun and a whole lot more useful to you if you are creative with the visual design as well as the features you include. Once you learn how to develop a website like this book suggests, you will be able to build on the basic concept and add features that you find useful.

It is intended that the reader read this book while seated in front of a computer rather than while relaxing in an easy chair. I will say it here and I will say it again to make sure that you understand, even though the code has been provided on the website as a reference, the code should be hand typed and the graphics should be created by hand. When the book calls for the reader to use a sheet of paper to draw the design or to answer some question, the reader should put pencil to paper and do as it says. Work through the examples. Read the code line by line. If at first you don't understand what the code is doing, read it again. All of the code is built on things you already know or will know by the time you reach it, so look for what is new and go from there.

Once you understand the code in the book, it will help if you write your own version of the same thing and then build on it by creating new things using the same concepts. Learn it however you can, but whatever you do, don't move forward until you understand each section.

I hope you will find this book helpful. If you do, please email me at the following address:

bookcomments@timothyfish.net

I would also appreciate being told of any websites you create using the concepts in this book. Also, if you feel so inclined, a link from your website to one or more of mine would be very nice.

Step 1:
Decide To Have A Website

*For which of you, intending to build a tower,
sitteth not down first, and counteth the cost,
whether he have sufficient to finish it?*
– Luke 14:28

There are many reasons for people to consider having a church website. Some may wish to give their church a presence on the internet. Others might desire to bring their church in to the twenty-first century. Still others might have a desire to communicate with church members or to provide a way for church members to collaborate. Some may already have a church website and need to find ways to improve it. Whatever has brought you to this point, the first thing that must take place in the development of a church website is that a church must make the decision that it needs a website. Either formally or informally a church must ask the question of whether the benefits of having a website justify the costs of having a website.

The Costs Of A Website

The costs of a website may include the funding for the website as well as the labor that is involved. Some large churches may be able to pay a company to build and maintain their website, but there is always somewhere else that the money could be put to good use. Medium and small churches may have little choice but to rely on volunteer labor. The amount of labor required to maintain a website can range from a few hours per year to one or more people working full time.

A website requires a server. Some organizations offer free or low cost server space, but for a quality website a church should expect to pay more than seventy dollars annually for server space. There are other expenses such as domain registration and software that push the bill higher. Even so, a church that budgets a hundred dollars a year and utilizes skilled volunteer labor can have a good website. Some churches may be able to do it for less, but this book assumes that a church can scrape together one hundred dollars.

The Benefits Of A Website

In many cases, the benefits of a good website can easily outweigh the cost of having a website. One of the benefits is that people looking for a church can find information about the church. In some areas there are hundreds of churches. A person moving into the area may visit a few churches that are near their home, but as they expand their search they are less willing to visit a church without additional information. A church website can provide them with enough information to make a decision on whether to visit the church or not. The church website can provide people with directions explaining how to find the church. The church website can provide contact information. These things, when added to other things the church is already doing can encourage people to visit the church.

A church website provides an additional medium through which church members can be kept informed. A calendar of events can be made available that lets people know what is happening. Members who missed a Sunday or misplaced their church bulletin might visit the church website to see what is happening during the week. It can provide information about ministries of the church. Some churches use their website to allow small group leaders to advertise their small group to other church member or even those outside the church. Some church websites make audio or video recordings of sermons available. A website can be used to allow people to sign up for various things. A website can be used as an online card catalog for the church library. The possibilities are nearly endless.

Because churches don't operate on profits and contacts don't equate to dollar signs, it is hard to put a value on the benefits of a church having a website, but the contacts a church can make through its website can range from a few hundred per year to several thousand. The people that walk through the church doors as a result of viewing the church website will likely be a small percentage of that. Churches that are located in sparely populated areas will tend to make fewer contacts through their website and churches that already have name recognition in densely populated areas will have more contacts. The majority of churches will fall in the middle.

A very important thing to consider when deciding whether to have a church website or not is that there is probably at least one person in your community that will look for information about the church on the internet. The internet is becoming the tool of choice in finding information about people, businesses and other organizations. Having a presence on the internet allows your church to have more control over what information is available.

One should not assume that every church should have a website. A website is a lot of work and it requires someone or a group of people to be willing to spend long hours working on it. If people are not available to do the work or those who are unable or unwilling to make the required commitment then it is better for a church to not have a website than to have a website that is poorly maintained. A website that is out of date or has links that are no longer valid gives the same impression as having boards over the church's windows would give a person passing by. A poorly maintained website makes it look like the church has closed its doors. This is not the impression that a church should be giving potential visitors.

The Website As A Ministry

The church website is more than a few pages of text and graphics on the internet. The church website is more than an electronic church bulletin. The church website is a ministry. The a good church website will touch people's lives and can minister to people that the church would never be able to contact by any other means.

The church website should live and grow with the church. A website is not something that can be checked off of a list once it has been put into place. A website is not like a church sign. Once the church sign is installed it can be checked off the list as being done, but a church website is never finished. There is always something that needs to be done. The calendar must be updated frequently. Photos must be added if people are to see them. An article must be written occasionally. If a Sunday school class has changed rooms then the class location information needs to be updated. When a new ministry is created the website must change. In a living church there will always be something happening that needs to be reflected on the website.

The web ministry of a church is partly an outreach ministry, it is partly a teaching ministry and it is partly a support ministry. There is the potential of touching more lives through the church website than through any other ministry, but don't expect it to solve all of your problems. The other ministries tend to be more effective on an individual basis than the web ministry. This is why it is important to recognize the support ministry aspect of the web ministry. Yes, it is possible to reach the lost and attract new members through the website and yes, it is possible to teach using the website, but there is no risk that the church website will replace the more traditional methods of doing these things. The real benefit of the church website comes in the way it can enhance the other ministries of the church.

One ministry that the web ministry might enhance is the Sunday school or some other small group ministry. Power-Point is becoming more prevalent as a teaching tool. A teacher might like to provide his PowerPoint slides to his students by posting them to the church website. The teacher might use a online application as a teach tool for his students to use during the week.

The pray ministry can also be enhanced. The Prayer Leader might like to make a dynamic prayer list available to the prayer warriors.

Another ministry might provide a list of things that are needed. As people make a commitment to provide each item the list would be updated. The possibilities of a church website are nearly limitless, so it is very important to consider the specific needs of the church and its ministries.

The most important part of any ministry is the impact it has on the lives of people. If the church web ministry is not going to have an impact on the lives of people then there is no reason for a church to waste time and resources developing it. If a church decides that it needs a website then those who are responsible for developing this ministry need to take great care to consider how it impacts the lives of others and what can be done to improve the impact it has on people's lives.

In making the decision concerning a website, a church must decide whether having a website will help it to accomplish its goals. A church needs to consider whether it has the resources needed to put a website on the internet and to maintain the site. A church needs to consider whether it has the volunteer labor needed or whether it will have to hire someone to do the work. This alone can make a big difference in the total cost of having a website.

Is It Worth It?

When everything is considered, many churches will come to the conclusion that the benefits of having a website outweigh the cost of having the website. If this is the conclusion to which you have come then this book is for you. In the pages that follow you will find a step-by-step approach that will take you from a state of having no website to having a website that meets your needs, is attractive and is easy to maintain.

If you already have a website you may find some sections that cover material that you already understand. Rather than skipping this material completely, please skim through it. You may find that some of the ideas presented here will help you to make improvements to your existing church website.

The Stone Chapel Church

Many of the exercises in this book are based around a fictitious church call *The Stone Chapel Church*. The exercise will take you through the steps of developing a website for this very average church. If the church actually existed it might be very much like your own church.

In the book you will find the code that is required to develop a website. The code is also available on book's website (*http://ChurchWebsiteDesign.TimothyFish.net*). To get the full benefit of the book you should ignore the code on the website and type the code in by hand. Anyone who has spent much time developing software will tell you that a great deal can be learned about a language by typing someone else's code into the development environment. This book requires action on your part. Even if you copy the code from the website you will need to write code to support your own website needs.

The Stone Chapel Church website is more than just a simple website. It is the basic framework that is needed to have a easily maintainable website. If you follow the examples with your own website then you will have a website that is a pleasure to maintain rather than a chore.

Step 2:
Select a Ministry Team

And let them judge the people at all seasons; and it shall be that every great matter they shall bring unto thee, but every small matter they shall judge. So shall it be easier for thyself, and they shall bear the burden with thee.

– Exodus 18:22

Soon after the children of Israel left Egypt Jethro went to Moses and saw the burden that Moses had. Moses was spending much of his time judging. Jethro recommended that Moses select men to carry out the task and only the most important things would make it up to Moses. The judicial system in the United States is based around this concept.

There are a couple of things related to Jethro's recommendation that apply to church website development. One is that Moses was trying to do it all himself and he was getting overworked. Church websites are often a one person task and there is no one to help when that one person becomes overworked. The other is that Jethro recommended a system that allowed for people to do what they knew how to do and to allow others to do the rest. The chosen men could judge what they knew how to judge, but if they didn't know then they would pass the case on to someone else. Eventually, Moses might ask God directly.

Working With What You Have

It is often the case that the person who will develop the church website and the person who is the biggest supporter of the church having a website are the same person. At the time of this writing, I am the webmaster for South Park Baptist Church in Fort Worth, Texas. I am not the original webmaster. When we first decided to have a website our associate pastor was a big proponent of the idea. After the church agreed it was he who set up the original website. My own contribute came later when other commitments made it impossible for him and others to properly maintain the site.

When working with volunteer labor it is not always easy to select the person who is the most qualified for the job. The person who is qualified may be unwilling or unavailable. The people who are willing may be unqualified. Often someone has a desire to develop a website, gets a small taste of HTML and assumes himself to be an expert webmaster. There is much more to developing a quality website than the ability use HTML tags. On the technical side, HTML has gotten to the point that even though it is essential it is almost a minor part of many websites. More than that, a quality website requires more than just the technical skills to code the website.

Since you are reading this book it is likely that you have some influence over who will be involved with the web ministry. You might be the designated webmaster and are looking for guidance on how to do your job. You might be a pastor, staff member or some other church leader who is trying to figure out what is needed to get your church on the web. Whatever the case, you have some influence in who will be involved.

When considering the personnel who will be involved, first look at the people who have expressed a willingness to be a part of this ministry. This might be one person. It might be you. Ask yourself some questions about this person. What skill does this person have? Does this person have any experience in developing a website? Are thess websites similar to what a church might need? Does this person have a history of following through on his commitments? Is this person grounded in the faith? Has this person demonstrated good taste and artistic ability?

A nice looking website requires that some artistic skill be used. A church website needs to have content that is created by people who are at least doctrinally sound enough to teach an adult Sunday school class. Some technical ability is a must.

Sometimes we run across people who are technically skilled, doctrinally sound and are artistic, but this seems to be rare. People with an interest in technical things are often not as aware of what things look nice. There is also the problem that technology tends to be the realm of the young but wisdom and doctrinal knowledge tends to come with age. This can be a problem, but it is one that can be handled.

If I could build a web ministry dream team I would have a minimum of three roles. In rare cases one person might fill all three, but it might require three or more people to fill all of the positions. The three roles are a ministry leader, a webmaster and an artistic director.

The Role Of The Ministry Leader

All successful ministries have someone who leads the ministry. Some are put in charge by a formal process like the vote of the church and some lead informally because of the respect of the other people working in the ministry, but there is always someone who is ultimately responsible or the ministry will fail from lack of direction.

The purpose of the Web Ministry Leader is to help the other workers work together. The ministry leader will also be responsible for determining what content should be permitted on the website and what content should not be there. For this reason it is important that the ministry leader be doctrinally sound. A person who does not understand and agree with the doctrinal statement of the church should not be allowed to serve in this role.

The Role Of The Webmaster

Because of the technical nature of website development, the webmaster is usually the first person chosen. The webmaster does the majority of the work that is required to develop and maintain a website. In this role a technical mindset is important. It is also important that the webmaster be willing to make a commitment and stick with it. Depending on the nature of the website, a webmaster may need to spend hundreds of hours a year working on the website. This is not a job that can be taken lightly.

Selecting the first person who jumps at the chance is not a good idea. The ideal person may be someone who is someone reluctant at first because he recognizes just how much work is required to do a good job. People who are anxious to take the job tend to have no idea just how much work is really required or they have the intention of producing a website that has very little use.

The Role Of Artistic Director

Though the web was once primarily about content, presentation plays a very important role in the websites that are available today. How the information is presented helps the user to know whether the information is worth his time or if he should move on to another page. An artistic director can help with this.

The role of the artistic director is to ensure that what is presented to the people viewing the website is attractive and not offensive. When some people learn of the fascinating things that can be done they want to try them all. There are many very ugly websites that have flashing text, moving images and blaring music. It is the responsibility of the artistic director to make sure that the webmaster pays attention to how things look instead of always looking fro ways to show off what can be done.

The Dividing Lines

The roles described above do not have to have a one-to-one correlation to the people involved. For the work I have done on the South Park Baptist Church website I have pretty much filled all three roles, but I frequently seek advice from other people. The role of webmaster is filled primarily by me, but some of the features of the website have made it possible for some of the responsibilities of that role to be parceled out to other people. I have a lot of control over the content of the site, but there are others who are actively involved in the decision making process. How your church fills these roles will be based primarily on who is available, the skills of these people and the content of your website.

Step 3:
Determine The Content

The cloke that I left at Troas with Carpus,
when thou comest, bring with thee, and the
books, but especially the parchments.
> – *II Timothy 4:13*

For a website, there is nothing that is more important than the content. In the early days of the internet content consisted of text and little else. As the internet has evolved, content can be many different things. For a shopping website like Amazon.com content is text, images and automated forms that allow a user to purchase the products online. For software companies like Microsoft® content is a sales pitch for their products and other related information such as product documentation and support pages. The content of a fan site is focused on the site owner's idol. There are even some sites where the content is nothing more than a list of links to other sites. In each case, the content is the most important part.

Some people are ideological and believe that the content of the internet should be limited to text. While there are some benefits to a text only site, the fact remains that most people grow tired of reading lengthy explanations. A good presentation is needed, but don't get too hung up on how to present the content yet. At this point you must decide what it is that you want to say to your audience.

In terms of the roles of the web ministry dream team, content falls within the role of the ministry leader. It is best if several people provide inputs, but in reality it is usually the webmaster and maybe a few other people who have the most say concerning the content of the website. It is always good to discuss these things with other people. The pastor and church staff is often a good place to start. Teachers and other church leaders should also be consulted.

Determine The Audience

It is impossible to know what you should say until you know something about what the audience needs to know. Think about the target of your website. Most church websites have a dual audience. Many churches hope their website will help to draw outsiders into the church, so part of the audience is people outside the church. Churches also like to provide information for people who are members of the church. There are so many differences between these two audiences that they must be handled somewhat differently.

Targeting Those on the Outside

The Stone Chapel Church is like many churches and one of their desires is to see their church grow. One of the reasons they want a website is to encourage more people to visit their church. The first thing they must consider is what these people are like. Some of these people have either moved into the area or have grown tired of the church they have been attending and are considering other churches. Some of these people used to attend a church, but now they have dropped out. Some of these people have seldom or never attended church and have no desire to start.

Those Seeking a Church

The people who are looking for a church are the easiest people in the target audience to reach with a website. There is a chance that these people will go to a search engine and type something like "churches in fort worth." If they have seen the church building they might even type something like "Stone

Chapel Church." What is it that a church would want to tell these people and what are these people looking for when they visit the site?

A good place to start is the church schedule. It is a very important piece of information. Not all churches start at the same time. Some churches have multiple services. A person visiting a church for the first time does not want to walk in late. It would be very embarrassing to walk in just as the pastor is finishing his sermon. Providing the times the church meets on the website allows people to find this information without driving to the church to get it from the church sign and without the person needing to call either the pastor or the church office.

Another important piece of information is the church's doctrinal statement as well as its associational or denominational affiliation. There is a trend among some churches to remove this information from their church signs. While there are good reasons on both sides of this debate, there are people who know what they believe and desire to find a church with similar beliefs. These people will find it very helpful to have information about a church's beliefs in a written form rather than having to attend the church several times only to discover that the church teaches something that they consider to be heresy. It is a waste of their time and a waste of the church's time.

People like to know what to expect when they are in a new situation. The church website is an excellent place to tell people what they can expect when they attend church. Do people dress up for church or do they wear casual clothes? What kind of music is sung? How long is the church service? There are many questions that might be answered. The Stone Chapel Church might have a statement similar to the following:

> *When visiting The Stone Chapel Church for the first time you can expect that some people will be dressed in "their Sunday best" while others will be wearing more casual clothes. The music style at the*

Stone Chapel is best described as blended. There is a mix of the older styles of music and the more contemporary styles. During Sunday school the children are taken to age specific classes and there are three classes for adults. One class is for ladies, one is for men and a mixed class meets in the auditorium. The worship service begins as 10:50 and usually dismisses just after noon. Please ask the greeter at the front door if you need to know where the nursery is located.

Take a break from reading and write a similar statement that describes your own church. While writing it, try to think of what your experience would be like if you were visiting your church for the first time. Perhaps you have had that experience. What was it like? You might consider asking someone who has recently started attending your church about his or her experience on the first day.

Contact information is also very important for people who are considering visiting your church. Is there an office phone number? What are the office hours? Is there a number that people can call when the office is closed? Are there e-mail addresses? Is there a van ministry? If there is, who should be contacted if a person needs a ride to church?

The location of the church is very important information to put on a website. You should also provide directions. Some churches are located on the busiest street in town while others are located on a side street. If the church is in a city then people might need directions no matter how busy the street is. It will do little good to tell people about your church if they don't know how to find it.

Those With No Interest

For those who have no interest in church it is a little more difficult. One would like to tell these people how to be saved and tell them that they should be in church, but the nature of the internet makes this difficult. It doesn't hurt to have a few things like this on a church website, since people would expect that a church website would be the source of this information, but don't expect very many people to look at this information. By its nature, the internet provides people with the information for which they are looking. Very seldom do lost people go to their computer and type in "what must I do to be saved?" If your goal is to reach people outside the church then your site must go where they are, in a manner of speaking.

What are people in your community doing if they are not interested in church? Are they farmers? Are they engineers? Do they hunt or go fishing? Do they do needle work? If you want these people to visit your site then give these people a reason. For example: you might provide information about where the fish are biting in your area. If the information is accurate then the fishermen are likely to start visiting your site just to get that information. While they are there you can tell them other things that you feel they really need to know.

Providing this information can help reach these people, but there is a danger in providing information that is unrelated to the church. If one is not careful the church website will no longer provide information about the church because it is providing so much information about everything else. One way to get around this is to create more than one website. One should be dedicated to church related information while the other is dedicated community information, but provides additional church related information. In the examples in this book we will ignore the community information, but for your website you may want to include it.

Targeting Those on the Inside

There are many factors that determine what information and services the church website should provide church members. As churches get larger each person knows less about each of the individual ministries of the church while in smaller churches it is almost impossible for someone to not know what is going on in most aspects of the church's ministry. Each church has different views about what information the members need and how to provide it to them. Some ministry leaders see benefits in providing information through the church website and others do not. It is the responsibility of the church web ministry to know what the specific needs of the church are and what it can do to provide for those needs.

One feature that is very useful is an online calendar. The calendar can keep people informed about what things will be happening at the church. If all of the ministry leaders are pro-active in seeing that all of their activities are included on the calendar then it can help them as they try to schedule events around other things. Some churches use online calendars to schedule shared resources such as classrooms, projectors, vehicles, etc. A calendar has the added benefit of providing those outside the church with information about the kind of activities they can expect.

Some churches provide audio or video recordings of services to shut-ins and others who request them. These same recordings can be provided via a church website. There is something of a limiting factor because not all people use the internet or have the bandwidth needed for access to large files, but having them available online makes it possible for people to listen without making a special request. Another possibility is to provide an order form for the available recordings in the church audio/video library.

Providing ministry specific information on the website can be very useful. This lets people know about the various ministries and can keep ministry workers informed. As an example, a ministry worker might check the church website to see if it is his turn to do something like mow the yard, clean the building, or teach a class. A ministry might provide a list of needs and church members can make a commitment online to meet these needs. As they do, the list would be updated and there would not be a duplication in effort.

A church only chat room or forum might be helpful in some cases. These might be used for the members of the church to discuss things without the need to call a meeting or to make phone calls.

Providing articles and useful links can also be helpful to church members. In providing articles and links, look for things that might help people as they serve the Lord. Some of this might be included in the ministry specific stuff, but some of it might be of a more general nature.

Many churches like to put pictures of activities on their website. This is primarily for church members. People outside the church will probably look at them if they happen to be at the site, but it is church members who will visit the site specifically to view them.

Deciding What You Really Need

There are many things that you can do, but how much do you really need? In making that determination ask the following questions:

- How will this benefit another ministry of the church?
- Are other churches doing this and how well does it work on their website?
- Will the people who have this information be proactive in providing it or will I have to ask them several times?
- Are there several people who will use this information or only a few?

If you are having trouble deciding what you need then you may find it helpful to hold a brainstorming session with the ministry leaders in your church. At this point, don't worry about how you will do these things, but come up with ideas on what you need. It is often hard for a webmaster to do this because he or she is constantly considering how to pull this thing off. If this is a problem for you then you might consider asking someone else in the church to facilitate a meeting in which people brainstorm for ideas about should be in the website. They may come up with a few ideas that aren't feasible. That is ok. You will have the opportunity to filter these things out later.

The Content For The Example

The Stone Chapel Church held a brainstorming session and decided that it needs the following:

- A brief description of the church
- The doctrinal statement
- A list of ministries
- Descriptions of Ministries
- A church calendar
- Visitor specific information
  - Directions to the church
  - Explanation of what to expect
  - Contact information
  - A statement on how people can be saved
- Photos of recent events
- Sermons online

This list will be seen again in the examples that follow. In an engineering environment we would write a requirements document based on this list. The requirements document would be reviewed by the stakeholders and would become something of a contract between the developers and the costumer. We don't need to be so formal, but we do need to have a clear idea of the direction we are headed. The later it is in the process when we add new features the harder it will be to make changes. At this point changes can be made by adding or removing a line of text, but after coding is complete the same change may require hours of work.

In the space provided on the next page or on a separate sheet, record the things you think your church website needs. You will be using this information later.

Why did you start to consider a website for your church?

What would you want those outside of your church to know about your church?

What could a website provide your church members to help enable them to do their jobs in serving the Lord?

Make a list of the things you think you need on your website:

Why did you start to ... or a website for your
...

... would you ... ... B? ...

When ... a web ... ... your ...
... in ... ... them ... ...

Write ... ... of ... ... you ...

Step 4:
Design The Website

Therefore whosoever heareth these sayings of mine, and doeth them, I will liken him unto a wise man, which built his house upon a rock:
– Matthew 7:24

If you have searched the web much while considering creating a website you may have noticed that there are many different companies and people who are willing to design your website for a price. The meaning they attach to design can range from selling you a template for you to fill in with your content to a complete turnkey job that gives you a completed website ready for the visitors you hope to have. For a business that finds that it has more money than it has qualified labor or a business that can't justify paying several times the price for their own qualified labor to create a completely custom design, these purchasable designs can be a very attractive option. For churches it is hard to justify going this route. Churches tend to have more people who are willing to do the work than what they have money to pay an outsider to do the same work, so as you follow along with this book you will find that it does not take this route.

Web design companies present some other problems as well. One problem is that there isn't enough room in the one hundred dollar budget to pay for even a seventy dollar template, much less a several hundred dollar turnkey job. Another problem is that many of these designs do not fit well with the methodology that is presented here, so they may be harder to maintain. It is also doubtful that you are reading this book so you can be told to let someone else do it.

Once we get away from the options that let someone else do the work, the term design takes on a whole new meaning. Designing a website is more than just deciding where all the pretty pictures go. Design includes that, but it also includes how we are going to present what we intend to say to the user, how this information will be stored on the server, what security must be in place to prevent unauthorized access and a number of other things.

Designing For Maintainability

The majority of the time that is invested in any website falls into the category of maintenance. Now, strictly speaking, software doesn't fail and doesn't need to be repaired, but these terms are often used because there are some similarities between the work that is done with software and a piece of equipment that wears out over time. Software fails when there is a preexisting flaw that is inadvertently discovered by a user. Because the developer didn't know about the flaw and assumed the software to be perfect it seems like the software failed even though it is doing exactly what he told it to do.

When software fails it becomes necessary to fix the problem. Software doesn't wear out over time but as time moves on some data become obsolete, there are changes in standards and many other things occur. With a website it is necessary to add new information, remove old information and even do things like change the appearance of the website to make it look fresh. All of this is considered maintenance. If a web developer doesn't want to spend all of his time doing boring work, the maintainability of the website must be considered as it is designed.

How Websites Are Designed

As software engineers think of the word, many websites are not truly designed at all. When they are complete they have a design, but frequently people skip the design phase and jump immediately into writing code. A person might decide that a column of links needs to go on the left side, a picture on top and a main body of text. He might produce something that looks a little like the following segment of code:

```
<!DOCTYPE HTML PUBLIC "-//W3C//DTD HTML 4.0 Transitional//EN">
<html>
<head>
<title>The Stone Chapel Church</title>
</head>
<body>
<DIV style="WIDTH: 680px; POSITION: relative; HEIGHT: 512px">
<DIV style="Z-INDEX: 101; LEFT: 0px; WIDTH: 120px; POSITION:
absolute; TOP: 88px; HEIGHT: 424px">
Ministries<br>
Contact Us<br>
Sermons<br>
</DIV>
<IMG style="Z-INDEX: 102; LEFT: 0px; WIDTH: 680px; POSITION:
absolute; TOP: 0px; HEIGHT: 88px" height="88"
src="P4243181.jpg" width="680">
<DIV style="Z-INDEX: 103; LEFT: 120px; WIDTH: 560px; POSITION:
absolute; TOP: 88px; HEIGHT: 424px">
Welcome to website of the Stone Chapel Church of Fort Worth.
</DIV>
</DIV>
</body>
</html>
```

Don't worry, for now, about what this HTML actually does other than it is a typical design of a web page. It really isn't important right now. The important thing to realize is that with about five minutes work this short segment was created and it could influence many aspects of the website for years to come. After successfully completing this page another page might be created that is just a copy of this page with a few modifications. After this page has been copied several times the person developing the website might realize that he really wanted to have "Contact Us" below "Sermons" and he also wanted to have a link back to the homepage on all of the pages. Depending on how this page was created, the software might correct the problems fairly easily or it may not.

Many people don't give any thought to how they are going to make modifications to the site until they are so deep into it that it is too late. A few luck out and the majority of their modifications are handled by whatever software they are using, but in many cases the method that was the easiest in creating the site is one that is the hardest to maintain.

My own experience as been that when a website is new it is easy to get caught up in the excitement of creating something different. I have a tendency to want to see my vision come to life quickly, even if that means skipping a few steps. I have found myself spending hours of my free time working on developing a website and it is hard to admit that the time will come that I will no longer be as excited about doing the work that is required. During the early stages there are so many things one wants to do, but when it all slows down there are fewer things that one wants to do and there seems to be more things that are a chore.

For example, it is easy to list an upcoming event on the homepage with the idea that at a later date it will be just as easy to remove it, but when that later date comes it is forgotten and other things keep the work from being done. The webmaster might not be thinking about the outdated event announcement, but the visitors to the site are sure to see it. The only thing it will do is let them know that the site is not being maintained. A site that isn't maintained will not get many return visits.

Reducing the Work To Make Changes

One of the things that can be done when designing for maintainability is to make the decision to reduce the work required to make changes to the site. Many servers allow server side includes. There is more than one way that this can be done, but most servers have some method of doing this. What this amounts to is that the server passes one file as part of another file. The text that is in the included file is treated no differently by the browser than the surrounding text, so it is possible to have one file that serves as a type of template while other files contain the details of the differences between the individual pages of the site.

A website might, for example, have a list of events on every page. The webmaster might need to make a change to the list of events. Instead of having to make changes to several pages with include files he only has to change one file to make the modification.

Include files are a big help, but having too many can add confusion. While trying to reduce the work of making modifications it is best to keep the number of include files down to a minimum. The ones that are used should be named in such a way that it is self evident what it does. If a file is intended to display copyright information on every page then it might be named something like "copyrightinfo.htm." If it is intended to show the navigation buttons on every page then "navigation.htm" might be a good name for it.

You will probably be the person who will be going back to make changes, but by the time you do you might as well be someone who as never seen parts of the website. The importance of comments cannot be stressed enough. This really fits more in line with the coding that will be covered in later steps, but the decision to have good comments is very much a part of the early stages of development. Without good comments you may have trouble understanding what you were doing and why you did it. Some code may be nearly duplicated in two or more places, so a change to one will need to be made to the others. Good comments will remind you of this and you won't be left wondering why the changes you made are not working.

Hiding files too deep in a directory structure can add confusion and increase the work of maintenance. A good directory structure keeps things separated, but having too many directories will just make it hard to find what you need.

Avoid changing the path to information. Even if the information has been archived make sure that it is accessed through the same path. In terms of maintenance, changing the path creates a problem because any hyperlinks to this information in your own site will no longer function after the path is changed and these hyperlinks will have to be updated. This can be a very tedious task. People who link to the information from other sites will also have trouble maintaining their sites and as you will see when we get to the topic of search engine optimization, this is one of the last things we want to do.

Let The Computer Make The Copies

While copy/paste can create big problems in maintaining a website, allowing the computer to do the copying on the fly can very effectively improve one's ability to maintain a website. Most of the major websites on the internet have some kind of database behind them. A database is just a convenient place to store many kinds of data. Calendars usually have a database behind them. Sites that have many different articles often have a database behind them. Blogs and forums have some form of database behind them.

With a database it is possible to use the same page to provide the user with data related to a specific query. For an example of a site that functions this way take a look at *http:// www.fortworthbaptistchurch.org/Articles/index.asp*. The articles on this page are stored in a database. There are links to a single page that retrieves the specified article from the database. This is based on the parameters. The big advantage of this is that it is possible to have hundreds of pages that are identical except for the primary content. If a change has to be made to the color scheme or the layout of the page it is a fairly simple change. Another advantage is that more than one style can be used to display the articles that are in the database. More than one site can even use the same data to target multiple types of users.

Design For Usability

Now is the time to begin considering how the website will actually appear to the user. Think of the computer monitors you have seen. Some are large, some are small and some are somewhere in the middle. Some users set their display so that everything appears big while others set it at a finer resolution. Some users are color blind. Some users can't see at all. This forces them to interact with their computer through sound.

When we start to consider factors like this we are beginning to design for usability.

If a site is hard to use, it can't be used with the user's computer or the user has a physical condition that prevents using the site then that user will not stay at the site very long. It is not always easy to think of every possibility, so even though we would like to have a site that is usable by everyone in reality there will be some who cannot use it. This may be because we didn't think of something or because we are unwilling or unable to handle the issue.

Make The Design Understandable

Think about what you would do if you walked into a dark room that you had never entered. The first thing you would want to do is to turn on the lights. You would probably feel for a light switch on either side of the door at about midway up the wall. There really isn't anything that makes it necessary to put the light switch in that location, but over the years people have learned to expect to find one there. The kitchen at our church has a light switch that is placed in an unusual spot. The light switch outside the door instead of inside. There is another switch inside that controls the garbage disposal. Many people have turned on the garbage disposal while trying to find the light switch. The problem is that the person who designed the electrical failed to consider the expectations of the users.

When it comes to a website there is nothing that prevents the designer creating a type of navigation system that is totally new. People who are developing a website for the first time have a tendency to want to try something different from everyone else, but most users just want to find a specific piece of information and get out. They don't want to have to e-mail the webmaster and have him explain how to find the information they need.

As with light switches there is a type of de facto standard when it comes to the operation of websites. Take a look at some major websites and you will notice that most of the navigational buttons and links are located along the left hand

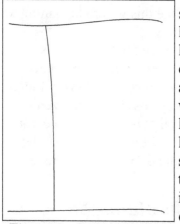

Figure 1—Initial Design

side of the page and some may be located along the top. There are links in other locations, but because so many websites are using a similar navigation system we would expect that most users will look for navigation links in these locations before they look at other sections of the page. Another thing that you might notice is that important information that is seldom used, such as copyright information and the webmaster's e-mail address are frequently placed at the bottom of the page. This prevents it from distracting from the rest of the information, but it makes it available to the user when needed.

We want a site that people will know how to use without being told, so let's begin by drawing out what we want. On a piece of paper draw a line about an inch from the top, another line along the left hand side below the first line and another line across the bottom. You will find that paper is easier to work with at this stage in the development process. You should have something that looks like Figure 1. It doesn't look like much but these three lines will serve as the framework for every page that is included in the website. When we add more to this you will begin to understand.

You will recall that Step Three called for making a list of things that are needed. The list for the Stone Chapel Church looked like the one on the right. Use your own list to determine what navigation links will go on the left side of the page. As you do, also think about how you might like to find this information if you are entering your website from the home page. Would you want all of this information on the left hand side or would you like a hierarchy?

There really is not right way and wrong way of doing this. Your aim is to provide links that the user understands quickly. You might consider looking at other church websites to see what they use to describe the same type of thing that you want to include on your own. For the Stone Chapel Church example I will be using five navigation links, Home, Visitors, Calendar, Ministries and Sermons. The Home like will take the user back to the site's homepage. The Visitors link will provide information specific to people who are not members of the church. The Calendar link will provide access to the event calendar. The Ministries link will provide information about the ministries of the church and the Sermons link will take the user to a page where he can listen to sermons or read transcripts if they are available. On the next page is an updated design showing these things.

Stone Chapel Church Website Needs

A brief description of the church
  The doctrinal statement
A list of ministries
  Descriptions of Ministries
A church calendar
Visitor specific information
  Directions to the church
  Explanation of what to expect
  Contact information
  A statement on how people can be saved
Photos of recent events
Sermons online

There are some other things as well. You will notice that the person filling the artistic director role has gotten involved with this version. The top will have a photo and some information about the church. The left hand column is now curved and the text in the main area will be curved to go with it. The little chapel in the circle could be a picture of the church building or something else, but something will go there. Even in this rough form the design is beginning to take shape and the beauty of it is that it only took a few seconds with a piece of paper and a pencil to produce this design. The design can be easily discarded and another one can be drawn just as fast.

For your own website incorporate the elements you want into your design. You can do something similar to the one for the Stone Chapel Church or you can come up with something different.

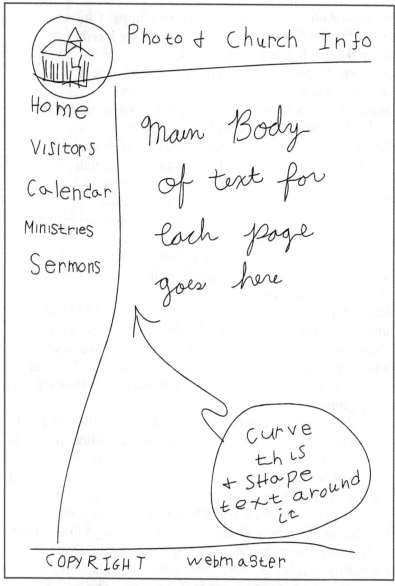

Figure 2—Second Design Iteration

Handling Important Information

If you have something that is important to say, do your best not to hide it. The information that people will be looking for when they visit your site should be available on the first page if at all possible. Things like meeting times and directions need to be on the home page or no more than one page away. We will be looking at how to do this later, but part of the design phase is thinking about where everything will go and how the user will find it.

There will be some things that you will want the user to see if he doesn't see any other thing. This kind of information should be placed prominently on the front page, but not in the same place where the navigation links are located. In the design we have so far there is a Main Body. This is where the most important information should go no matter what level of the website it is in. On the home page it might contain meeting times and a description of the church. On the Visitors page it might contain a message to people who might be considering attending the church. On the Ministries page it might be a list of the ministries. Each page has important information for the people who are looking at that level.

Incorporate The Church

One of the things that I like to do when I am developing a church website is to pull features into the site that are a part of the church. In this case, when I say church I don't mean just the people, but also the church building, the property where the building is located or even elements of the community. In creating a church website it is like we are trying to capture a snapshot of the church. We can't package the whole church and deploy it to a web server, but when people look at the web site we want them to see the church in much the same way that one might see a friend while looking at a photo. We want to put our best foot forward, but at the same time we don't want them to be shocked when they visit the services.

Make the Website Look Like the Church

One thing that can be done is to make the website look like the church. Take a close look at the church. What might a first time visitor notice about the church? What distinguishes the church from some other church? Are there large carved doors gracing the entrance? Are there flowers that are blooming? Is there a ornate stained glass window? Is it a cowboy church with lots of hay bales lying around? Is there something distinctive about the exterior like a bell tower or an unusual steeple? Is there a duck pond or a fountain? Is there a creek running across the property? Is there a color scheme that runs throughout the building? What features would really stand out the most to a visitor?

Use the most prominent features in the graphical design of your site. This is a little like a caricature of the church. By pointing out the most memorable features we can make something that looks nothing like the church look very much like it. A visitor to the site will remember having seen these features when he drives past the building or when he walks through the door. This reinforces his memory of having seen both the building and the website.

Find Elements To Incorporate

Many churches have a color scheme to their building. South Park Baptist Church in Fort Worth has a lot of maroon that is very prominent. Because it stuck so well in my memory I incorporated it into the design of the website. The things that should be incorporated will often stand out, but sometimes they don't.

Suppose what really defines the church to visitors is something other than what can be seen. Maybe there is something different about how the church conducts small group Bible study. Maybe what stands out is that the church has people from many different ethic groups. Maybe the church is friendlier than most. It is not enough to put a statement on the website saying "we are a friendly church." What reason would a visitor have to believe that? Find a way to show this friendliness on the website.

One way to handle things like this is to use quotes from people who have visited the church and then later joined. Ask people why they joined the church. Ask what made the church different form other churches. Post the answers to the website. Several quotes from church members is more believable than a statement by the webmaster.

Look for things that are not as obvious. Is there something about the staff members or the other church leaders that sets them apart from the average church leader? Have some of them graduated from seminary? Do they have experience that makes them uniquely qualified to do their job? A church website is not exactly the most comfortable place to be boastful of such things, but if people are looking for a reason to go to one church over another they want to know these things.

Elements That Shouldn't Be Included

Not everything that can be included in a website should be include. The web is a very public place and when information is placed on a web page it has the potential of being accessed by people who will use it for purposes other than what was intended. There are some things that should not be included on a website so that there is no danger of people using this information in the wrong way.

Churches are filled with hurting people with problems. People often go to church because they have reached the end of their rope and they are looking for help. Some people have health problems, some people have lost their job, some people are having marital problems and the list goes on. People often ask for prayer and these prayer requests end up on a prayer list. One might think that a prayer list is something that should be included on a website. People from the church could check the list on the website from time to time and know who needed prayer. The problem is that prayer lists include some information that is really quite confidential in nature. The people who put their names on these lists usually have the belief that only the church will be seeing the list. While churches generally don't guarantee this, it is best not to make this information too widely available. If it is made available on a website it should be password protected so that access to the information can be tightly controlled.

Most big businesses take big steps to protect their proprietary data and the sensitive data of their customers. The U.S.

Government has even higher levels of protection. Unlike the government and businesses, churches and religious organizations tend to operate on the assumption that they have nothing to.

   Some time ago I found myself in a very uncomfortable situation because of information that was made public that should have been protected. Some of the information that I post to our church website comes from another website that has given permission to copy some of the articles on it. One of these articles originated from information made public by the Missions Department of an association of which our church is a member. The article gave the name of a missionary that would be working in a country that is almost completely closed to the gospel. I copied the article verbatim and posted it to our website. Sometime later I received a letter from a gentleman mentioning that the missionary had told him and others that the ease of finding the missionary's name and the name of the country with internet search engines was a major concern. He requested that I remove the article from our site. By that time it was too late to prevent the problem, but I did as he asked. I did so because I felt it would make him feel like he had done something to help remedy the situation, but any damage that had been done was already done. A few weeks later the missions department made public what they had done to remedy the situation. By making this information public they may have put themselves in the same situation as before. I couldn't help but wonder why they would make information available that might hinder the efforts of a missionary and even put the missionary in danger of government action if the foreign government became aware of it. I have not reported this additional information on our website, but it seems likely that it will be available to anyone who wants to find it.

   Reporting contact information can also be a problem. Some people might not want their telephone number or address made readily available. There are other places to get this information, but as a matter of policy I try not to list any personal addresses or telephone numbers. E-mail addresses are another thing that can be a problem. Any e-mail address that appears on a webpage is a prime candidate for unsolicited e-mail.

It is necessary to provide e-mail addresses so people can make contact through the website. Rather than providing the e-mail address a staff member normally uses, create an address that is part of the domain. One of the domain names our church has registered is *spbcfw.org*. All staff members have an address at this domain. There is also an e-mail address for the church office. It is *office@spbcfw.org*. People who want to contact the church will always be able to use this address even if the church has to change ISPs or if the church secretary quits.

Concerning Copyrights

When considering what should and shouldn't be included in a church website, copyrighted material is a big no-no. Every webmaster will have to deal with a copyright issue at some point. Some people have some misconceptions concerning copyrights.

One misconception is that if it doesn't say it is copyrighted then it isn't. The vast majority of original material that is in a fixed form is considered to be copyrighted from the time the author created it. Fixed form basically means that it is stored as a hardcopy or in a machine retrievable format somewhere besides in someone's head. If you aren't sure if something is copyrighted it is best to assume that it is.

Another misconception is that it is legal to copy copyrighted material as long as it is not sold. Copying anything that is not in the public domain or for which you do not have permission from the copyright holder is illegal. It doesn't matter whether you are making money from doing so or not. Look at it this way. Suppose a coffee shop was selling coffee at fifty cents a cup with free refills. A customer goes in, pays his fifty cents and gets a cup of coffee. Someone else comes in. Rather than paying for his own cup of coffee he brings his own cup and the first person pours the coffee into the man's cup then goes and gets a free refill. This continues with several more people. Even though the customer is not making money, the coffee shop is losing money. This is similar to what happens when a person copies intellectual property and provides it free, without permission, to other people. The copyright laws are designed to protect copyright holders from this.

Can I Use What I Download?

Web browsers often make it all too easy to borrow intellectual property from other websites. The most popular web browsers allow the user to view the HTML source. It is a nice feature to have, but it can be temping to copy someone else's work. It is also easy to grab images either through the Save As capability or by taking a screen shot.

In most cases, the HTML, the images or the other files that you might obtain through the methods mentioned cannot be used in your own website. If the copyright owner has explicitly given you permission to copy his work then you are permitted to copy as much as he has permitted you to copy, but if it is just something that you happened to see and decided you liked then by including this data on a church website you are putting yourself and your church in danger of a lawsuit.

Files that are intended to be downloaded generally have some kind of statement describing what is acceptable use. Pay special attention to license agreements and statements on sites concerning downloads.

Live By A Higher Standard

What does it really matter? Most people aren't going to bother to sue someone for copying their work, right? Churches should operate by a higher standard than what most businesses do and yet there are many churches that will compromise on this issue because they don't want to pay fees to gain permission to copy the data. Some might be willing to pay the fees, but they have chosen to remain ignorant concerning the issue. We may make a few mistakes, but we should void using intellectual property without permission.

We should especially try to avoid using it in our church websites. It is bad enough if clipart is inadvertently used in the church bulletin without permission but it is much worse if stolen images or text is placed on the church website for the whole world to see.

Exceptions To The Rule

As a general rule, anything that you didn't create should be treated as if it is copyrighted material and copyrighted material should not be used without the copyright owner's permission. As with anything there are also exceptions. U.S. Copyright Law includes exceptions for fair use and works of the U.S. Government.

Anything that is created by the U.S. Government is in the public domain. That doesn't mean that everything is publicly releasable. There are other laws that protect data that would present a danger if it was made available to enemies of the United States of America. The United States Government creates massive amounts of data each year and, in keeping with first amendment rights, any of this data that is not classified can be used in pretty much any form.

The exception for fair use is a little more complicated and at times it is very unclear. The courts have handed down many decisions in favor of people who have used copyrighted material when certain conditions were met. Much of this has to do with the balance of first amendment rights with the right of people to protect their intellectual property and other private data. According to the U. S. Copyright Office in an online document FL-102, "Although fair use was not mentioned in the previous copyright law, the doctrine has developed through a substantial number of court decisions over the years. This doctrine has been codified in section 107 of the copyright law." (www.copyright.gov/fls/fl102.html, July 2006) It goes on to state that there are various purposes for which the use of copyrighted material may be considered to be fair use. Specifically it mentions criticism, comment, news reporting, teaching, scholarship and research. In making a determination there are four factors to consider. These are the reason for its use, the nature of the work, how much is used and the effect on the market. If you want to be certain it is best to consult a lawyer, but let me tell you what I think this means.

Some of the information that is included in church websites falls within the things protected by fair use. Websites often criticize and comment. A church website may do some news reporting and teaching. So there are some things that can be included on a church website without the copyright holder's permission, but there are also many things that cannot be include. The fact that a church is nonprofit organization does not automatically give it permission to disregard a person's copyright protection.

To me, the intent of the fair use section seems to be that the right of the people in a democratic society to be informed outweighs the right of a person to copyright protection, but there are still limitations. Suppose your site includes an article that is critical of something that was posted on the website of a church in another denomination. The law seems to protect your right to make comments on the post and to include portions of it on your own website for the purpose of making those comments clear. Now suppose that the same website had a photo that you liked and thought might look nice as the background for your own website. Fair use does not permit you to use the image without the consent of the copyright owner in this case. Fair use also does not prevent them from taking you and your church to court. It only gives you some very limited protection if you are taken to court.

Purpose and Character of Use

The Copyright Office states that the first of the four factors to be considered is "the purpose and character of the use, including whether such use is of commercial nature or is for nonprofit educational purposes." (FL-102, 2006) Ask yourself why you want to use the material. Are you doing so because you seek to gain from it or because you believe people need to be informed. For example, suppose you find a recipe. One reason you might want to place this recipe on a website is to increase the traffic flow to your website. Another reason might be that there is something wrong with the recipe and people need to know. The first use would probably require permission while the second may not.

The Nature of the Copyrighted Work

Another factor to consider is the nature of the copyrighted work. Hymn books are copyrighted. Many of the songs within them are also copyrighted. An entertainer is prevented from performing these songs without permission, but when a church buys hymnals they expect to be able to sing these songs during their worship services without paying an additional fee. Because of this expectation we can generally assume that all that is required to use these songs in this way is to buy the book ,even though many hymnals do not have an explicit statement that the songs can be used in this way. The nature of a hymnal does not carry over into the use of a song on a website. While it may be ok to use streaming audio or video of live church services that include songs that are copyrighted, having recordings of these songs may not be permitted. Carefully consider the nature of the work and what people expect to be able to do with it.

Amount Used

The third factor to consider is how substantial the amount of the material is compared to the whole of the work. If you copy a few lines of an author's work, give him credit and make comments on it then you may well be protected by the fair use section. On the other hand, if you copy a whole copyrighted poem or article and place it within your own work then you are probably just asking for a lawsuit and you would probably lose. Fair use allows for you to make a point with copyrighted material. What it doesn't allow you to do is to use the work of someone else and treat it like your own.

Market Impact

The effect that the use of copyrighted material has on the potential market for the work is also something that is considered in issues of fair use. One of the problems that the entertainment industry has is that some people will make illegal copies of movies and music which they sell at a reduced price or which they provide free over the internet. This has the potential of reducing the amount of money the copyright owners can make on their work. On the other hand, a fan might create a site that contains the lyrics of the songs on a CD. This could actually increase the popularity of the CD and increase the market potential, but it might reduce the value of a book containing the lyrics and music, so fair use is questionable in this case. The cover design of an author's book is copyrighted, but showing this cover on a website along with a recommendation to buy the book would likely increase the value of the book, so this would likely be considered fair use.

Given the uncertainty concerning whether the use of copyrighted material is fair use, it is best to get permission. Some companies spell out on their websites how their data can and cannot be legally used. Some of what they permit is simply a restatement of the copyright fair use policy. If you want permission that extends beyond that then you may have to pay a fee or simply not use it.

For more information about the laws concerning copyrights please visit *www.copyright.gov*.

More Design Work

Software design is more of an art than a science. There is often a question of just how much must be documented and how much can be left to the next phase of the work. In a business environment people often have an perception that software design work is the work that it takes to produce the several hundred page design document required by the company's software development process. Some people will spend many days producing this document while others will spend a great deal of time talking about how they wish it didn't have to be done. In cases where the design team and the implementation team are the same people the design document may not be used and it is a chore to update it after the software is implemented.

What can get lost in these types of situations is that the purpose of the design has more to do with communication and keeping us on track that what it has to do with producing a document. It doesn't matter what fancy tools are used and what methods are used to document the design if the design does not tell the implementation team what it needs to do or if it is so lengthy that the implementation team doesn't have time to read it.

Fortunately, most churches don't have strict guidelines on how software development is to be done and church websites do not have to be very complicated. In looking at what you need for a sufficient design, consider who will be using the design. In most cases it will be you.

If you had hired a company to design a custom website for you then you would expect that they would show up for a design review with more than just a sheet of paper with some lines and some scribbled text. Most likely they would have the graphics in place, the links would be hot and there would be sample text in place. Even for us it might be good to do some of this work. If you need to present your idea to your church before they approve spending money on it, having this kind of stuff in place makes it easier for people to see what they will be getting.

Before we get into detailed design, there are some things that need to be added to our pencil drawing design. We need a rough idea of what we want in each of the main pages of our site. What do we want to display in the body of the home page? What do we want to display to visitors? What are the ministries? Since we expect that the people coding the pages and the people designing them are the same, we would expect that we could put this off until we get to the details, but it is better to do it here. Once we get into detailed design we will be much more focused on technical details than on how things look and what things should be included. If, in detailed design or coding, there is something does doesn't seem to be working there is a temptation to just accept the position in which something happens to be rather than continuing to search for a way to accomplish what the design specifies. If

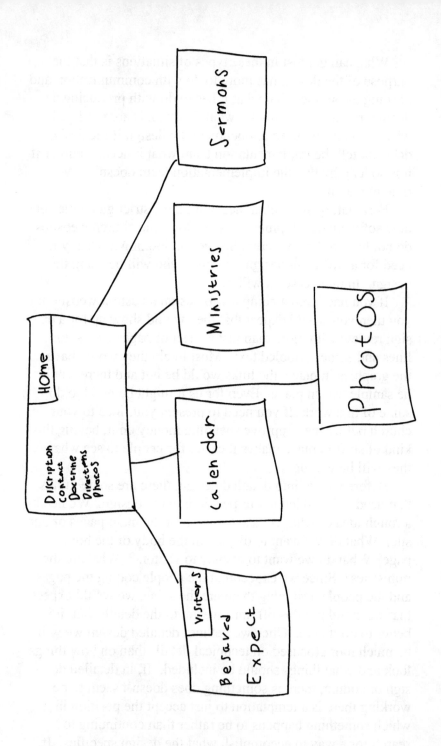

Home

Discription
Contact
Doctrine
Directions
Photos

Sermons

Ministries

Calendar

Photos

Visitors

Be saved
Expect

the design doesn't specify something then we are more likely to accept what we get.

Pull out the list of needs that your church has for a website once again. Look at the things that are not included in the things that you included on the navigation bar. Ask yourself which navigation link you would expect to click in order to get to this information. Make a table that looks something like the one below:

Need	Page
Description of Church	Home
Doctrinal Statement	Home
Descriptions of Ministries	Ministries
Calendar	Calendar
Directions	Home
What to expect	Visitors
Contact Info	Home
How to be saved	Visitor
Photos	Home
Sermons	Sermons

Make another drawing that looks similar to the one on the opposite page and reflects the items that are in your own table of website needs. The boxes are pages on the site and the lines indicate that a link will take us from the home page to these other pages. In actual fact these pages will all be inter-linked, but there really is no need to show that here. The words within each box provide enough information to tell us what will be included on each page. This is really all we need at this point. The rest of it will begin to fall into place as we begin to develop the framework in the detail design phase and eventually begin writing code that will tie these pieces to-gether.

If you have more information or information that should be on lower level pages you can draw them in on your own drawing as well. The drawing that I have included here is intended to only be an example. Many church websites have several more levels. You decide what works best for your church.

Step 5:
Learn the Tools of the Trade

*Then Simon Peter having a sword drew it, and
smote the high priest's servant, and cut off his
right ear. The servant's name was Malchus.*
– John 18:10

If this is your first time to develop a website then you
have very little experience working with some of the tools
that are needed to develop a website. There are many different methods that can be used to develop a website and sorting
through all of them to help you decide which ones to use and
which ones to ignore is one of the major purposes of this
book. This book is not intended to be a complete reference on
any of these technologies. There is not a lack of documentation for the technologies that are available to create websites.
The web has thousands of pages that are dedicated to this purpose. There are also book companies, like O'Reilly & Asso-
ciates, that have a many different books that document many
aspects of internet technology. This book is intended to give
you a starting place and to help tie some of the pieces together. Once you have put some of this technology to use it
will be much easier for you to understand the rest of it and
how it all comes together into an integrated whole.

The primary focus, here, will be on Extensible Hypertext
Markup Language (XHTML), Cascading Style Sheets (CSS),
Active Server Pages (ASP) and a little bit of JavaScript, SQL

and Microsoft® Access™. You will find many differing opinions about which technologies to use, but the most important thing we will be concerned with here is how to tie these technologies together into a single website. Before we can be very concerned about that, you need a basic understanding of what each of these are.

Extensible HyperText Markup Language

Extensible HyperText Markup Language or XHTML as it is more commonly called is part of the technology that has given us the ability to follow links from one page to another, to see text in bold, underlined or italics and even to see images displayed on pages. XHTML is the latest HTML and is intended to replace it, in time. If you already know HTML then you won't have any trouble picking up XHTML. If you don't know HTML then you are at an advantage because you haven't had a chance to pick up some of the bad habits that those of us who have been using HTML for several years have. We will focus on XHTML 1.1 here because it is the latest released standard for HTML. The X comes form the term XML which is the Extensible Markup Language. XHTML is a combination of XML and HTML. The term *hypertext* is drawn from its ability to provide *hypertext links* though they are more frequently called *hyperlinks*. The term *markup* is drawn from the fact that tags are added to the text of a document. XHTML tells the browser what elements the author has placed in his document but it doesn't tell the browser how he wants the document to be displayed. The author might intend for the title to be large, the main text to be in the Arial font, portions to be in italics and for there to be an image that illustrates his point.

What XHTML doesn't do is guarantee that the user will see the data in exactly the way the author intended. A user's browser may be a different size. The user's browser may handle tags differently than what the author would like. There are many reasons why the output may look different than ex-

pected. Some users can't see, so their browser reads to them
instead.

Exercise 1: A Simple XHTML Document

There really is no better way to learn what XHTML is all
about than to jump right in and start using it. To do this you
will need a text editor and a web browser. Notepad will work
fine for the text editor and the web browser can be your normal browser of choice. You might also consider installing a
tool like Amaya™, available at *www.w3.org/Amaya/*, which
will allow you to edit XHTML 1.1 code and see the results in
the same application. I recommend creating a new folder to
hold the files you will be creating as you work the exercises in
this book.

Create a new text file named "Exercise 1.html" and open
it with the text editor. The "html" extension will tell your operating system that this is a HTML file and should be sent to a
browser. In the text editor, type the following then save the
file:

```
<?xml version="1.0" encoding="utf-8" ?>
<!DOCTYPE html PUBLIC "-//W3C//DTD XHTML 1.1//EN"
    "http://www.w3.org/TR/xhtml11/DTD/xhtml11.dtd">
<html>
        <head>
        </head>
        <body>
        </body>
</html>
```

Go ahead and double click on this file to bring it up in the
browser. You should see a browser window that has no text
or graphics displayed in the area where you would normally
see a webpage. Select View Source from the menus and you
should be able to see the source of the page. It should look
very similar to what you typed into the text editor.

<!DOCTYPE> Tag

Before we look at anything interesting, let's look at the
four tags that are in this document. The first is the <!
DOCTYPE> tag. Mostly you can ignore this tag. Many web
developers have gone for years without giving this tag much

thought, but these beginning statements specify which version of the standard you are using in your document. If you use Amaya™ it will fill this in based on the inputs you give it when you create a new XHTML file. Browsers are very forgiving and may not say anything if you don't even use the lines before the **<html>** tag, but you should place them here anyway.

If you look at this tag closely you will notice that *xhtml11.dtd* is being used. Using version 1.1 of the XHTML standard will help to insure that we are using HTML as it was intended by defining what the content is and not how it is to be presented. It is necessary to validate a XHTML document. You will find out about this later. You will also notice "w3c" and "www.w3.org" in the tag. W3C® is the trademark of the World Wide Web Consortium. They are the organization that is responsible for the XHTML standard and other things.

<html> Tag

The next tag is the **<html></html>** tag set. This signals the browser that everything between the opening **<html>** tag and the closing **</html>** tag is HTML. As you create a document you will put everything between these two tags, but other than that you can pretty much ignore them.

<head> Tag

A XHTML document has two major sections a head and a body. The head is surrounded by the **<head></head>** tags. The information that is included between these tags is not intended to be displayed by the browser. There are five tags that can be used within the head of the document, **<base>**, **<link>**, **<meta>**, **<script>**, **<style>**, and **<title>**. We will come back to these later. The head generally includes information that is descriptive of the document as a whole.

<body> Tag

The body is where the information that is to be shown to the user is located. It is surrounded by the **<body></body>** tag set. Any of the XHTML tags that have not already been mentioned can be used between these tags, but before we try those, insert a line of text between the body tags and save the file. The file should have something like the following where the body is located:

```
<body>This is the body of an HTML file.</body>
```

When you open the modified file in a browser you will see a line of text like the one above without the tags. The body is were the author tells the users what he wants them to know.

<base> Tag

As was stated above there are five tags that can be used in the head of the XHTML document, **<base>**, **<link>**, **<meta>**, **<script>**, **<style>**, and **<title>**. The **<base>** tag tells the browser where the relative URLs on the page are based or located. A page might be located at *http:// TheStoneChapel.TimothyFish.net*. The images might be located at *http://www.TimothyFish.net/Images/*. If a base is specified then specifying an image as "Image01.jpg" for the **<img>** tag would tell the browser to look for this image at *http://www.TimothyFish.net/Images/* rather than at *http:// TheStoneChapel.TimothyFish.net*. An example of doing this is as follows:

```
<head>
<base href="http://www.TimothyFish.net/Images/" />
</head>
```

Notice that the **<base>** tag ends with "/>" in this case. Any tag that does not have a matching closing tag must end in this way. This is a shorthand form for closing the tag.

\<link> Tag

The **\<link>** tag describes the linkage between the XHTML file and another file. This tag is frequently used with Cascading Style Sheets. You will be using this tag some in developing your church website. The following is an example:

```
<head>
<link rel="stylesheet" type="text/css" href="style.css" />
</head>
```

\<meta> Tag

The **\<meta>** tag gives information about the document to search engines, browsers and people reading the code. It can also set the refresh rate of the page. Many search engines use the description that is provided by one of these to provide the description that is displayed in the search results. At one time keywords could be added to one of these tags to let the search engines know that the page could provide information about a specific topic. Most search engines have stopped using these. You will find an explanation of what search engines use instead when we cover the topic of search engine optimization.

\<script> Tag

The **\<script>** tag allows a script, often JavaScript or VBScript, to be inserted into the XHTML document. Scripts are a powerful feature because they can run on the user's machine rather than running on the server. A script can be used for things like checking for valid input before a form is submitted or obtaining information about the user's machine and settings that can then be used to determine what should be displayed on the user's machine.

\<style> Tag

The purpose of the **\<style>** tag is to define a style that is specific to the page. Styles that are used throughout the website should be defined in a Cascading Style Sheet and linked through the **\<link>** tag. This is covered in more detail in the topic concerning Cascading Style Sheets. A style specifies how elements of the document should be displayed. If for some reason you wanted all bold text on the page to be red then you could use the following:

```
<style type="text/css"><!--
b {color:red}
--></style>
```

The <!-- ... --> seen here is for comments. This is for the benefit of people with older browsers that don't recognize style sheets. This is optional because there are very few people with browsers that will not know how to handle this.

<title> Tag

The <title> tag gives a name to the web page. Take a look at what your browser is displaying at the top for the example we created earlier. Mine displayed something like *D:\My Documents\Exercises\Exercise 1.html*. Now add a title to the head. The example should now look something like the following:

```
<?xml version="1.0" encoding="utf-8" ?>
<!DOCTYPE html PUBLIC "-//W3C//DTD XHTML 1.1//EN"
    "http://www.w3.org/TR/xhtml11/DTD/xhtml11.dtd">
<html>
<head>
<title>Church Website Design-Example 1</title>
</head>
<body>
<p>This is the body of an <b>HTML</b> file.</p>
</body>
</html>
```

After making this change you will probably see something different when you load the file into the browser. Now put some more of the tags to use and make Exercise 1 look like the following:

```
<?xml version="1.0" encoding="utf-8" ?>
<!DOCTYPE html PUBLIC "-//W3C//DTD XHTML 1.1//EN"
    "http://www.w3.org/TR/xhtml11/DTD/xhtml11.dtd">
<html>
<head>
<meta name="description" content="Church Website Design: A
step by step approach - Exercise 1" />
<title>Church Website Design-Example 1</title>
<style type="text/css">
```

```
b {color:red}
</style>
</head>
<body>
<p>This is the body of an <b>HTML</b> file.</p>
</body>
</html>
```

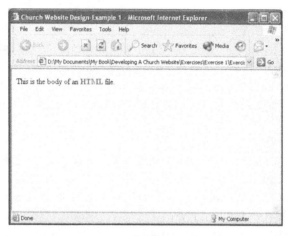

The **<p></p>** tag set makes the enclosed text a paragraph and the **<b></b>** tag set makes the enclosed text bold.

Validate the Example

The last thing that needs to be done with this example is to validate the XHTML. The World Wide Web Consortium has a tool for validating HTML and XHTML. To access this tool go to *http://validator.w3.org*. Under "Validate By File Upload" click browse to find the file from the exercise on your hard drive. Click "Open" and then finally click "Check." Hopefully, it will come back and state that the page is valid. Using this tool will help to reduce the unexpected results that may come from a browser if there are non-standard elements in the XHTML file. However, it will do nothing for browsers that do not fully implement the standard.

Exercise 2: Creating the Document Text

When thinking about what should go into the body of the XHTML document, think more about what you want to say and less about how it should be presented. This is not always easy to do. Some of the things we put in web pages are more about presentation than anything else. We expect a calendar, for example, to look a certain way so we start thinking about the presentation first.

Suppose you were copying a passage from the Bible into an XHTML document. Some Bibles have the words of Jesus written in red and the words that the translators added in italics. Suppose you wanted to make your document look similar. The first thought might be that you would like a tag for red text and a tag for italics. There is a tag for italics but not for red text. There is a reason for this.

A better understanding of the problem is that you want to mark everything that Jesus said and everything that the translators added and then specify that the browser should display Jesus' words in red and the words the translators added in italics.

There are many tags that can be used in the body of a XHTML document. While the presentation tags are now deprecated it is still not quite as clear that some of the tags are describing the content rather than specifying how to display the content. If you find yourself using a tag because you know it will make something look a certain way then you need to rethink what you are doing.

Attributes

XHTML tags often have several attributes. Some of them are optional and some are not. Many of the attributes are specific to the tag while there are others that are used by many of the tags. Some attributes that are available in nearly all

XHTML tags are shown in the table below:

Attribute	Usefulness
Class	Identifies the class for formatting purposes.
Id	Provides a unique identifier so the element can be referenced by other tags.
Style	Inline style that allows one time style changes.
Title	Used when tool tip style help is desired for the element.

In Exercise 1 the **<meta>** tag and the **<style>** tag used attributes, but not the ones in the table above. In this book you will see the *class* attribute used frequently and it is one that you would use frequently in writing your own XHTML pages.

To help you understand why you might want to do this, suppose you have created a page with several hyperlinks. Some links are of interest to men and some are of interest to women. You might like to distinguish between the two sets. The *class* attribute makes this possible. You will find that more reasons for using this attribute will become apparent as you work through the exercises in this book.

The Exercise

In the same way you created an XHTML file for Exercise 1, create a file called *Exercise 2.html*. In this exercise you will learn how to create the text of an article that might be included in a website. It will have the typical things including headings, hyperlinks, bold, italics and images.

Suppose the pastor of the Stone Chapel Church wants to write an article telling about two new series of sermons that he will be preaching. It might look like the following:

Two New Sermon Series

Beginning in May I will be begin preaching two new series of sermons. In the morning services I will be preaching from I John and in the evening I will be covering the book of Nehemiah.

Series I: How to know that you are saved

The book of I John was written so that we could be certain of our salvation. During this series of sermons I will be presenting several proofs that you can use to determine if you are truly saved. **Do you know that you know?**

Series II: How to be a leader

The book of Nehemiah gives us an example of how God used a man to lead a people to greatness. In this series we will be looking at how Nehemiah led in rebuilding the wall and how we can all be better leaders.

The article might have appeared in the church bulletin and the webmaster wants to make this available on the website. XHTML is a markup language, so he marks up the church bulletin a little before he starts writing XHTML.

There are three paragraphs in the article, a main heading and two subheadings. There is also a sentence that is in bold. Based on his markings he develops the XHTML code:

```
<h1>Two New Sermon Series</h1>
<p>Beginning in May I will be begin preaching two new series
of sermons. In the morning services I will be preaching from I
John and in the evening I will be covering the book of
Nehemiah.</p>
<h2>Series I: How to know that you are saved</h2>
<p>The book of I John was written so that we could be certain
of our salvation. During this series of sermons I will be
presenting several proofs that you can use to determine if you
are truly saved. <b>Do you know that you know?</b></p>
<h2>Series II: How to be a leader</h2>
<p>The book of Nehemiah gives us an example of how God used a
man to lead a people to greatness. In this series we will be
looking at how Nehemiah led in rebuilding the wall and how we
can all be better leaders.</p>
```

Two New Sermon Series *Heading*

Beginning in May I will be begin preaching two new series of sermons. In the morning services I will be preaching from I John and in the evening I will be covering the book of Nehemiah.

Series I: How to know that you are saved *subheading*

The book of I John was written so that we could be certain of our salvation. During this series of sermons I will be presenting several proofs that you can use to determine if you are truly saved. **Do you know that you know?**

Series II: How to be a leader BOLD

The book of Nehemiah gives us an example of how God used a man to lead a people to greatness. In this series we will be looking at how Nehemiah led in rebuilding the wall and how we can all be better leaders.

In using what you learned in Exercise 1 place this code in *Exercise 2.html* between the **<body></body>** tags. You should have something that looks similar to the following:

```
<?xml version="1.0" encoding="utf-8" ?>
<!DOCTYPE html PUBLIC "-//W3C//DTD XHTML 1.1//EN"
   "http://www.w3.org/TR/xhtml11/DTD/xhtml11.dtd">
<html>
<head>
   <title>Church Website Design-Example 2</title>
   <meta content="Church Website Design: A step by step ap-
proach - Exercise 2" name="description" />
   <style type="text/css"></style>
</head>
<body>
<h1>Two New Sermon Series</h1>
<p>Beginning in May I will be begin preaching two new series
Of sermons. In the morning services I will be preaching from I
John and in the evening I will be covering the book of
Nehemiah.
</p>
<h2>Series I: How to know that your are saved</h2>
<p>The book of I John was written so that we could be certain
of our salvation. During this series of sermons I will be
presenting several proofs that you can use to determine if you
are truly saved. <b>Do you know that you know?</b>
</p>
<h2>Series II: How to be a leader</h2>
<p>The book of Nehemiah gives us an example of how God used a
```

```
Man to lead a people to greatness. In this series we will be
looking at how Nehemiah led in rebuilding the wall and how we
can all be better leaders.
</p>
</body>
</html>
```

When you load this exercise into the browser you might
notice that it doesn't look the same. There may be fewer lines
than you were expecting. The headings are not the same size
as the original and the subheadings aren't in italics. If you
happen to know something about HTML you might think that
the thing to do is to add the **<i></i>** tag around the subheadings. This would work or another option would be to replace
the two **<h2>** tags with two **<h2 style="font-style:italic">**
tags, but we will use neither of these. If you were posting this
to a forum that accepts HTML input then these options would
be fine and maybe even ideal, but going into this we are making the assumption that our goal is to create a website rather
than a single page. This is covered in more detail in the section on Cascading Style Sheets but for now just replace **<!--
h2 { font-style:italic} -->** between the **<style></style>** tags.
This will cause the **<h2></h2>** tags to function the way we
want. Any addition subheadings in this file will be displayed
consistently. We will ignore the size of the font for now. The
"problem" we just encountered is a part of how the web is
supposed to function. XHTML only tells the browser what
things are. Before spending a lot of time beating your head
against the monitor because the browser doesn't show your
XHTML document like you wanted , remind yourself that
XHTML describes the content and not the way it should look.
If you can remember this then developing a website will be a
whole lot easier. XHTML relies on the style to tell the
browser how to display something or whether to display anything at all. Even then it is only a suggestion and the browser
is free to display things the way the user and the browser developer intend rather than how the webmaster intended. In
the case of the **<h2></h2>** tags, they are there to tell the
browser that something is a second level heading and not that
the text is to be larger than normal as some people assume.

Hyperlinks

The **<a></a>** tag or anchor tag is used to create a hyperlink within an XHTML document. The primary parameter for this tag is the *href* parameter which specifies the URL the browser is to access if the user clicks on the link. The following is an example of its use:

```
<a href="http://www.TimothyFish.net">Visit My Site</a>
```

Try your own hand at this. Add a hyperlink to the exercise 2 file so that "Series I" and "Series II" become links to some other website. The code for the "Series I" link might look like the following:

```
<h2><a href="www.timothyfish.net">Series I:</a> How to know
that you are saved</h2>
```

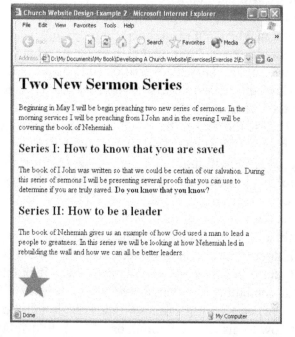

Images

Images are added to a document through the use of the **<img/>** tag. This tag has no ending tag, so use the closing shorthand notation. There are two attributes of special interest, *src* and *alt*. The *src* attribute specifies the location of the image and the *alt* attribute specifies text that can be displayed by browsers that do not display images. It is a good practice to always use the *alt* attribute. For the Vision Impaired People (VIPs) and for the benefit of search engines.

You can add an image to *exercise 2.html* by adding the following just before the closing **</body>** tag:

```
<p><img src="star.jpg" alt="blue star" /></p>
```

Alternatively, the image can be placed in one of the existing paragraphs. The source attribute can specify a file that is in a relative location to the XHTML document, or it can specify a URL were the file is located.

Exercise 3: Creating a List

As with the previous exercises, you will need an *exercise 3.html* file. If you like you can copy and rename the one from Exercise 2. The body will be different but the rest will remain nearly unchanged.

In writing, we often need a list. You will find lists in several different places in this book. The needs that were defined for the website that is being developed in this book is a multi-tier list. Some lists are numbered. Some lists are bulleted. Some are just a list. We use lists in our writing so often that we don't really think about them, but they help to group things together so that they are more understandable. XHTML 1.1 has three types of lists. They are as follows:

- **<dl></dl>** — Definition List
- **<ol></ol>** — Ordered List
- **<ul></ul>** — Unordered List

Definition List

As its name implies a Definition List has items that have a Definition. Two special tags can be nested in the **<dl></dl>** block. The **<dt></dt>** tag is used to indicate a term. The **<dd></dd>** tag is used to indicate a definition. To show how this works, put the following into the *exercise 3.html* file body:

```
<dl>
        <dt>Dog</dt><dd>Hairy animal that barks.</dd>
        <dt>Cat</dt><dd>Hairy animal that purrs.</dd>
</dl>
```

Ordered List

An ordered list is one where the order in which the items appear is important. These lists often have numbers or letters to indicate that order is important. In XHTML, the **<li></li>** tag is used to designate a list item. To try an ordered list, add the following to the *example 3.html* body:

```
<ol>
        <li>Breakfast</li>
        <li>Dinner</li>
        <li>Supper</li>
</ol>
```

You will probably have a list numbered from one to three. I say probably because how it is numbered is part of the formatting rather than the content. A browser or a style could number this list from A to C and still be consistent with what we have told it so far.

Unordered List

An Unordered List is the kind of list that normally has bullets to distinguish between list items. Add the following to the example file to see how Unordered Lists work:

```
<ul>
  <li>Apple</li>
  <li>Orange</li>
  <li>Grape</li>
</ul>
```

Nested or Sub Lists

Lists can be nested within each other to create sublists. The following example shows how this works. Add this to *example 3.html.*

```
<ul>
<li>Level 1_A
  <ol>
  <li>Level 2_A_1</li>
  <li>Level_2_A_2</li>
  </ol>
</li>
<li>Level 1_B
  <ul>
  <li>Level 2_B_1</li>
  <li>Level 2_B_2</li>
  </ul>
```

```
</li>
</ul>
```

As you can see, the nested list can be of a different type than the parent list. This is not a normal practice, but if you have data that would be represented this way, XHTML will allow you to do so. You can also continue nesting lists, so it would be possible to create an outline using these lists.

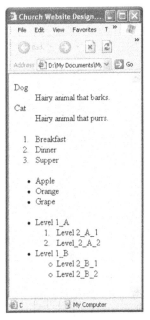

Exercise 4: Creating a Table

A table provides a way to present information in a form that is easily accessible to the reader. XHTML has several tags that make it possible to define a table. One of the easiest ways to explain how to create a table is to show you. Create a new file, like before, for this exercise. Name the file *exercise 4. html.* Add the following to the body of the file:

```
<table border="1">
<caption>Exercise 4 Table</caption>
<tr><th>Book</th><th>OT/NT</th><th>Chapters</th></tr>
<tr><td>Genesis</td><td>OT</td><td>50</td></tr>
<tr><td>Ruth<</td>td>OT</td><td>4</td></tr>
<tr><td>Romans</td><td>NT</td><td>16</td></tr>
</table>
```

Similar to the way lists are defined the **<table></table>** tag shows where the table begins and where it ends within the content. The *border* attribute specifies the width of the border. A value of zero would be used for a table with no borders. The **<caption></caption>** tag makes it possible to give the table a caption.

Tables have rows and the beginning of a row is indicated by the **<tr>** tag. The header row can and should be treated differently from the rest of the rows even if you expect it to be formatted in the same way as the rest of the table. Each heading is designated by a **\<th\>** tag. For the ordinary data of the table the **\<td\>** tag is used.

More to Learn

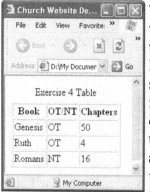

There is a lot more to XHTML than what has been covered here. Some things, such as forms, you will be learning as you work through the steps of this book that lead to a working website. Others will not be covered because they are not relevant to the goal. Documentation is readily available on the internet. The *www.w3schools.com* website has a wealth of free information concerning many website development subjects. Once you have figured out how some of this technology fits together you will find the information provided there to be very useful. You will find a listing of all of the tags that are available to you in Appendix A of this book.

Cascading Style Sheets

Cascading Style Sheets are used to define how the content of the XHTML document will be displayed. It is still up to the browser and user whether this takes place, but by using style sheets it is possible for the XHTML author to make his intentions known and even to define separate styles for different types of web browsers. The PC can display a different view than a web enabled phone. A page that has a lot of navigational things might print on a printer without anything except the main text.

The Basic Syntax

Style sheets have *rules*. A *rule* is a statement that defines how an XHTML element will be displayed. The XHTML element to which a *rule* applies is identified by the *selector*. The *selector* matches an XHTML tag. For example, one of the tags that was mentioned in the last section is the **<p></p>** tag. A *selector* for a rule that specifies how paragraphs are displayed would be **p**. *Pseudo-elements* or specific states of an element can be handled. The **<a></a>** element has several states. The state is given after a colon. *Selectors* can also be named to match the *class* attribute of an XHTML element, in which case they are preceded by a period.

The *rule* sets the *value* of a *property*. The *property* comes first which is followed by a colon and the *value*. The following is the basic syntax of a *rule*:

```
selector { property: value }
```

A *rule* can have more than one *property/value* pair per *selector*. CSS is not case sensitive.

How It Is Used

Styles are defined in four places. These definitions cascade down to the next level. If the next level has a new definition then the new definition is used, otherwise the previous definition is used. The first place styles are defined is in the browser defaults. As web developers, we have no control over these settings. The user has some control, but we have none.

The next place is in *external* style sheets. *External* style sheets are a separate file from the XHTML file that contains a set of CSS rules. Because it is separate file it can be used to define *rules* for more than one page on the website.

After *external* style sheets comes *internal* style sheets. These are *rules* that are defined in the **<style></style>** tag of the header. These rules apply only to the document in which they are located. They may replace *rules* that were defined in the *external* style sheet or the browser default.

The last place where styles are defined is the *inline* style sheet. *Inline* style sheets are defined as an *attribute* of a XHTML element. These style sheets modify only the element in which they are defined.

While writing and using style sheets it is best to try to avoid *inline* style sheets and to use *internal* style sheets sparingly. Defining style sheets close to the XHTML creates a risk of introducing inconsistencies in how the website looks and it also makes it more difficult to change the theme of a website.

Keep the scope of what you are doing in mind when you decide where to the *rule* should be defined. If the *rule* is an exception to the general layout of a page then it is best to place it in an *inline* style sheet even though it would be better if exceptions were not required. If the *rule* is an exception to the layout of the website or if it would not make sense to have the rule apply to more than one page then it should be defined on an *internal* style sheet. If the *rule* applies to two or more pages or even might apply to two or more pages in the future then it should be *external*. Keep in mind that each individual *rule* or *property/value* pair should be considered for where it should be placed. Do not place a *rule* in a particular spot because there is already a *selector* in that location. Make it a goal to write as few *rules* as you can to define all of the *rules* you need for the entire website.

Exercise 5: My First "Website"

If you have stayed with me this long then you have enough knowledge to put together a "website" on your local computer. It won't be a true website because we haven't gotten to the step that will explain what you need to do to make it available for the rest of the world to see and it won't be as easily maintainable as what later steps will tell you how to make it, but you do have enough knowledge to put together a collection of XHTML pages that are interlinked.

In this example we will make it seem more like a website because we are going to have multiple pages that have a consistent theme. This will demonstrate some of what is possible with CSS and things will become much more clear than a simple definition of CSS could make it.

For this exercise you will need to create a separate folder to hold the files that you will be creating. The first file you will need is *index.html*. Create this file in the same way that you created the other exercise files. Before you look at the code that is printed here, consider how you might reproduce the following as an XHTML file:

```
+---------------------------------------------------+
|                                                   |
|  Bible Quotes                                     |
|                                                   |
|      •  Isaiah 61:1-3                             |
|      •  Luke 4:16-22                              |
|                                                   |
|                                                   |
|                                                   |
|                                                   |
+---------------------------------------------------+
```

Creating the Site

The following is the code from an XHTML file that will produce similar results in the *index.html* file:

```
<?xml version="1.0" encoding="utf-8" ?>
<!DOCTYPE html PUBLIC "-//W3C//DTD XHTML 1.1//EN"
   "http://www.w3.org/TR/xhtml11/DTD/xhtml11.dtd">
<html>
<head>
   <title>Church Website Design-Example 5</title>
   <meta content="Church Website Design: A step by step
approach - Exercise 5" name="description" />
   <link rel="StyleSheet" href="style.css" type="text/css" />
</head>
<body>
   <h1>Bible Quotes</h1>
   <ul>
      <li><a href="isaiah.html">Isaiah 61:1-3</a></li>
      <li><a href="luke.html">Luke 4:16-22</a></li>
   </ul>
</body>
</html>
```

Your browser will probably handle this fine, but to make this file work the way it was intended you need another file called *style.css*. Look closely at this code and you will see that it is making use of the **<link>** tag. In reading the attributes of the tag you can see that a style sheet named *style.css* is being linked. Since this file does not currently exist in the folder you have created you will need to create it. To do this, create a text file called *style.css* in the same folder as *index.html* and but the following code into it:

```
/* Exercise 5 Style 1 */
body { font-family:Arial;
       background-color:White;
       color:black}
A:link {text-decoration: none; color:Blue;}
A:visited {text-decoration: none; color:Blue; font-
weight:lighter}
A:active {text-decoration: none; color:Blue;}
A:hover {text-decoration: underline; color:Navy; font-
weight:bold}
.Scripture { font-family:Arial;
                 font-size:larger;
                 color:Maroon}
.VerseNumber { font-size:large }
.JesusWords { color:Red }
```

Now when you load *index.html* into your browser it should look like the following the image on the left. The links have nowhere to go, so you will have to add a couple more files, but first take a look at what is happening here. Line one of the CSS file is just a comment. It is ignored by the browser, but it is always a good practice to make comments to remind you why you did what you did. This is especially important for larger files. The second line is the start of the body rules. There are three *pairs* here. The first specifies that the Arial typeface will be used. The second specifies the background color. This is the default color for some browsers, but not all and we want to make sure that the user sees white. The third *pair* sets the font color to black. So the result is that any text in the body will now default to black Arial on a white background.

In *index.html,* the next four rules specify how the Hyperlinks will appear. The first is how the user will see the link if it has not been visited. We set the *text-docoration* to *none*. This tells the browser not to underline the link. By these rules, only on *hover* will there be an underline. Hold your mouse over one of the links to see what happens. It is also set to change the color and display the link in bold. This and many other things can be done with style sheets.

The *isaiah.html* file that is needed for this exercise is as follows:

```
<!DOCTYPE html PUBLIC "-//W3C//DTD XHTML 1.1//EN"
  "http://www.w3.org/TR/xhtml11/DTD/xhtml11.dtd">
<?xml version="1.0" encoding="utf-8" ?>
<html>
  <head>
    <title>Church Website Design-Example 5:Isaiah</title>
    <meta content="Church Website Design: A step by step
    approach - Exercise 5" name="description" />
    <link rel="StyleSheet" href="style.css" type="text/css" />
  </head>
  <body>
    <div class="Scripture">Isaiah 61:1-3</div>
    <div class="Passage">
    <p><span class="VerseNumber">1</span>The Spirit of the
    Lord GOD is upon me; because the LORD hath anointed me to
    preach good tidings unto the meek; he hath sent me to bind
    up the brokenhearted, to proclaim liberty to the captives,
    and the opening of the prison to them that are bound;</p>
    <p><span class="VerseNumber">2</span>To proclaim the
    acceptable year of the LORD, and the day of vengeance of
    our God; to comfort all that mourn;</p>
    <p><span class="VerseNumber">3</span>To appoint unto them
    that mourn in Zion, to give unto them beauty for ashes,
    the oil of joy for mourning, the garment of praise for the
    spirit of heaviness; that they might be called trees of
    righteousness, the planting of the LORD, that he might be
    glorified.</p>
    </div>
  </body>
</html>
```

This file will produce output similar to the image on the next page. Notice the special formatting of the scripture reference. Also notice that the numbers of the verses are larger than the rest of the text.

The *luke.html* file that is needed for this exercise is as follows:

```
<!DOCTYPE html PUBLIC "-//W3C//DTD XHTML 1.1//EN"
"http://www.w3.org/TR/xhtml11/DTD/xhtml11.dtd">
<?xml version="1.0" encoding="utf-8" ?>
<html>
  <head>
    <title>Church Website Design-Example 5:Luke</title>
    <meta content="Church Website Design: A step by step
    approach - Exercise 5" name="description" />
    <link rel="StyleSheet" href="style.css" type="text/css" />
  </head>
  <body>
    <div class="Scripture">Luke 4:16-22</div>
```

Isaiah 61:1-3

1The Spirit of the Lord GOD is upon me;
because the LORD hath anointed me to
preach good tidings unto the meek; he hath
sent me to bind up the brokenhearted, to
proclaim liberty to the captives, and the
opening of the prison to them that are bound;

2To proclaim the acceptable year of the
LORD, and the day of vengeance of our God;
to comfort all that mourn;

3To appoint unto them that mourn in Zion, to
give unto them beauty for ashes, the oil of joy

```
<div class="Passage">
<p><span class="VerseNumber">16</span>And he came to
Nazareth, where he had been brought up: and, as his custom
was, he went into the synagogue on the sabbath day, and
stood up for to read.</p>
<p><span class="VerseNumber">17</span>And there was
delivered unto him the book of the prophet Esaias. And
when he had opened the book, he found the place where it
as written,</p>
<p><span class="VerseNumber">18</span>
<span class="JesusWords">The Spirit of the Lord is upon
me, because he hath anointed me to preach the gospel to
the poor; he hath sent me to heal the brokenhearted, to
preach deliverance to the captives, and recovering of
sight to the blind, to set at liberty them that are
bruised,</span></p>
<p><span class="VerseNumber">19</span>
<span class="JesusWords">To preach the acceptable year of
the Lord.</span></p>
<p><span class="VerseNumber">20</span>And he closed the
book, and he gave it again to the minister, and sat down.
And the eyes of all them that were in the synagogue were
fastened on him.</p>
<p><span class="VerseNumber">21</span>
<span class="JesusWords">And he began to say unto them,
This day is this scripture fulfilled in your ears.</span>
</p>
<p><span class="VerseNumber">22</span>And all bare him
witness, and wondered at the gracious words which
proceeded out of his mouth. And they said, Is not this
Joseph's son?</p>
</div>
</body>
</html>
```

There isn't a lot here that you haven't seen already. The **<span></span>** tag is being used to distinguish the verse numbers and the words of Jesus. In this case the words of Jesus are being displayed in red as one who has grown accustomed to reading a red letter edition of the Bible might expect. The class is used in the style sheet to specify specific formatting for these things. You will be using the **<div></div>** tag with style sheets to position the text in these pages differently than they currently appear, but first, let's look at how powerful style sheets can be in allowing us to change the appearance of a webpage without the need to modify all of the files.

Modifying the Site

Rename the CSS file *style1.css* and create a new one named *style.css*. This time put the following text in this file:

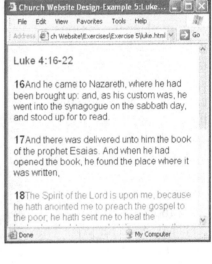

```
/* Example 5 Style 2 */
body { font-family:Arial;
          background-
color:Black;
          color:Gray}
A { color:White }
.Scripture { font-
family:Arial;
                  font-
size:larger;
                  color:White}
.VerseNumber { font-
size:small }
.JesusWords { color:White;
                  font-style:italic }
```

After you have finished typing in this code, reload *index.html*. From there you will be able to click on the links to load the other two files as well. You will notice that a drastic change has taken place. The background is no longer white. The verse numbers are smaller than they were before. The words of Jesus are now in white rather than in red. The whole site has been modified in such a way that the look and feel are totally different. Even though the entire site has been changed it only took a few changes in one file.

With some careful planning as you design and build your site, you can make it possible to change the appearance of even a much larger site with no more effort than what you had to put into modifying this small site made up of three files. The key is in making sure that you consistently keep the content separate from the presentation and that you appropriately tag each of the elements in the content.

You were able to modify the verse numbers and the color of the words of Jesus because the **<span></span>** tags were in place to handle these changes. Had they not been in place the options would have been much more limited. It is your responsibility, as a content creator, to make sure that the tags that are in place correctly describe the content, whether you are writing the content using a text editor or writing content using a tool that creates the XHTML code for you. The guy who created the XHTML editor has no idea what you might use it for

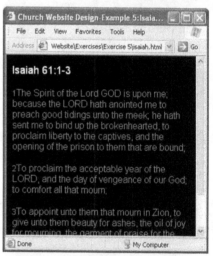

and cannot do more than make a few educated guesses about what tags might be useful. In many cases, it seems, too many tags are generated in hopes that some of them will apply. This makes the XHTML code very difficult to read. In other cases the styles are defined too close to the XHTML code and style sheets lose there effectiveness.

Effectively used style sheets are one way to reduce the amount of maintenance that is required. During the design phase it may be hard to imagine that one would want to change how things look, but over time it becomes evident that changes will need to take place and these changes need to be consistent across the site. The text size might be too small for some users to read. The colors may not look as great as they once did. From time to time one might decide that a fresh look would be nice.

On Changing Colors

There is a tendency to expect that what we see is what the user sees. We might be happy with our browser's default settings except we want the links to be Green instead of Blue or something like that. After adding a line to the CSS file that makes this one change we are happy with our results, but there is a problem. We want the site to be viewable by others, but the defaults on a user's machine may be different than our own. The user might have a Green background and his links might be White. By changing only one value we may be making it impossible for him to see the links on the page. To correct this problem, if you make any change in one of the colors then you will need to make a change in all of the default colors. This means writing rules that specify the same values that you have for the default colors in your browser.

Often images that are chosen for a website have colors that clash or do not look good with a different background. The best that can be done with this is to choose some images that will work with any background and be prepared to modify or replace the rest when there is a need to change the design of the website. In some cases it might be possible to have multiple versions of images available for an eventual or a dynamic style change. Style sheets can be used to select a set of images that work with the style settings.

Setting Positions

Before finishing this exercise, you need to do one more thing that will help you understand as you begin developing your church website in later steps. Copy *style.css* and rename it *style2.css*. In *style.css* put the following:

```
/* Example 5 Style 3 */
body { font-family:Arial;
       background-color:White;
       color:black}
A:link {text-decoration: none; color:Blue;}
A:visited {text-decoration: none; color:Blue; font-
weight:lighter}
A:active {text-decoration: none; color:Blue;}
A:hover {text-decoration: underline; color:Navy; font-
weight:bold}
.Scripture { font-family:Arial;
```

Device Specific Style Sheets

The web pages you create will be viewed by many differ-ent devices. The most common are probably the screen and the printer. When a user sees an article on your website that he wants to save for later or reference offline he might send it to the printer. One thing he probably doesn't want, or you don't want for him, is the graphic and navigation links that are on the page. By creating device specific style sheets it is possible to show the fancy graphics on the screen while dis-playing only well formatted text on the printer.

There are a couple of ways this can be done. One method can be used with external and internal style sheets. This method to encapsulate the rules in media type specifiers like the following:

@media screen { .JesusWords { color:Red } }
@media printer { .JesusWords { color:Black} }

Another way is by defining separate CSS files and using the <link /> tag to distinguish between them like this:

```
<link rel="StyleSheet" href="style.css" type="text/css"
media="screen">
<link rel="StyleSheet" href="print.css" type="text/css"
media="print">
```

```
                font-size:larger;
                text-align:right;
                color:Maroon;
                position:absolute;
                width:25%;
                border-style:none
                }
.Passage { width:60%;
                position:absolute;
                left:30%;
                border-style:dashed
            }
.VerseNumber { font-size:large }
.JesusWords { color:Red }
```

This is a variation on *style1.css,* but you will find that the browser displays something that is very different from either of the previous views. When the XHTML files were created they were created with two section or divisions. This was done using the **<div></div>** tag. One division was for the scripture reference and the other was for the passage. By default the browser will display these in flow order. One division will flow into the next and unless something is specified differently it will appear as normal. CSS makes it possible to reposition these divisions like an editor might reposition articles in a newspaper.

In this case, both divisions were set with absolute positions and their widths are set relative to the width of the browser window. Absolute positioning causes them to display some distance from the top left hand corner. The passage division is positioned 30% of the width from the left. Use *static* positioning to have them function as they did before and *relative* positioning to have them positioned some distance from where they would have been positioned if *static* positioning was used.

Positioning is set using *left, top, right* and *bottom* for either a *relative* or *absolute* position. *Left* in this case means the distance the left side of the element is moved from normal rather than to move the element some distance to the left.

When you get to the section that covers implementing your website, you will learn more about positioning elements using CSS. You will also be learning some techniques that

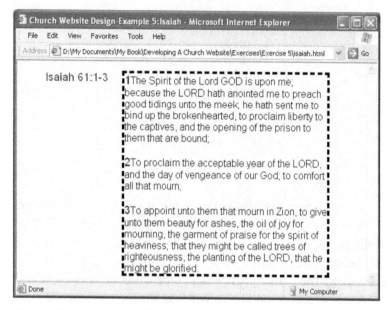

Isaiah 61:1-3 1The Spirit of the Lord GOD is upon me;
because the LORD hath anointed me to preach
good tidings unto the meek; he hath sent me to
bind up the brokenhearted, to proclaim liberty to
the captives, and the opening of the prison to
them that are bound;

2To proclaim the acceptable year of the LORD,
and the day of vengeance of our God; to comfort
all that mourn;

3To appoint unto them that mourn in Zion, to give
unto them beauty for ashes, the oil of joy for
mourning, the garment of praise for the spirit of
heaviness; that they might be called trees of
righteousness, the planting of the LORD, that he
might be glorified.

will enable you to use positioning to make your website do some very nice things.

There are many more aspects of CSS than what can be covered in detail within a book of this scope. More information about CSS is available in Appendix B. There are also many sources available online if you need information that is not provided in this book.

Server Scripts

So far you have seen some of the power in being able to change the appearance of a website with only a few lines of code. Imagine how much power would be at your finger tips if you could make modifications to the website without changing any lines of code, if input from the user changes the information made available to him, if the site provided different information based on the date, time of day or what other websites say and if the website could provide automated answers to some queries.

If you have spent even a little bit of time surfing the web then you know that all of these things are possible. The power that makes these things possible is server scripts and the *Common Gateway Interface* (CGI). The focus here is on server scripts and in particular ASP. While CGI provides more flexibility in the choice of a programming language, this book is intended for an audience that I believe to be more interested in creating a website than what it is in using a language like C++, Perl, Ada or some obscure language that has some special ability to handle a particular task. Server scripts are easier to work with for people who are generally not programmers.

The Hypertext Transfer Protocol is designed in such a way that a user, though the use of a browser, makes a request and the server sends a document. The browser displays this document and the user makes another request by clicking a button or a link. This process continues throughout the entire session. A server script is a script that runs on the server after a request is received but prior to the server sending the information that was requested by the user. If, for example, the user sent two values 304 and 875 to the server then the server could return the sum of these values (1179) or the product of these values (266,000) or even the number of entries in a database that have between 304 and 875 characters in a field, but servers are very dumb until someone tells them what to do. Server scripts are one way of telling a server that it is supposed to do something rather than just ignoring the user's input, like they do if left to their own devices.

There are several different server scripting languages including ASP, JSP, PHP and ColdFusion. Server scripts are a type of programming language as opposed to a markup language, but they have similarities to markup languages. All of the tags that are in XHTML are also in these languages. To these tags is added tags that encapsulate the code of the programming language. The XHTML tags are passed through but the server processes the additional tags and the code therein to produce additional XHTML to pass back to the user's machine.

Active Server Pages

Active Server Pages (ASP) was created by Microsoft®. It runs well on Windows® based servers and handles Microsoft®

Access™ databases easily. By default is uses VBScript as the scripting language but others, such as JavaScript, can be used.

ASP files have the extension *.asp* and are an XHTML file with code added. Below is an example of a very simple ASP file that is based off of one of the files created in *Exercise 5*. To create the ASP file create a file like you did with the XHTML files, but instead of the *html* extension use an *asp* extension for the file. You can save it in the *Example 5* folder so that all of the needed pieces are there even though you won't be able to see it work until is it on a machine with an internet server running on it.

```
<!DOCTYPE html PUBLIC "-//W3C//DTD XHTML 1.1//EN"
    "http://www.w3.org/TR/xhtml11/DTD/xhtml11.dtd">
<html>
<head>
  <title>Church Website Design-First ASP</title>
  <meta content="Church Website Design: A step by step
    approach - First ASP" name="description" />
  <link rel="StyleSheet" href="style.css" type="text/css" />
</head>
<body>
  <h1>Bible Quotes</h1>
  <ul>
    <li><a href="isaiah.html">Isaiah 61:1-3</a></li>
    <li><a href="luke.html">Luke 4:16-22</a></li>
  </ul>

  <p><b>Value of 304 + 870:</b> <%=304+875%></p>
</body>
</html>
```

In this you will notice one new thing:

```
<%=304+875%>
```

This does nothing more than add the two numbers. The code shown here is replaced with the value 1179. If you were to open an ASP file and view the source from the browser you would see no <%...%> tags. For this example it would look like the following:

```
<!DOCTYPE html PUBLIC "-//W3C//DTD XHTML 1.1//EN"
    "http://www.w3.org/TR/xhtml11/DTD/xhtml11.dtd">
<html>
<head>
  <title>Church Website Design-First ASP</title>
```

```
<meta content="Church Website Design: A step by step
    approach - First ASP" name="description" />
<link rel="StyleSheet" href="style.css" type="text/css" />
</head>
<body>
  <h1>Bible Quotes</h1>
  <ul>
    <li><a href="isaiah.html">Isaiah 61:1-3</a></li>
    <li><a href="luke.html">Luke 4:16-22</a></li>
  </ul>

  <p><b>Value of 304 + 870:</b> 1179</p>
</body>
</html>
```

There are many things that can be done with ASP. As we
look closely at what you need to do to build a church website
we will be covering the subject of ASP in more detail. Primarily this will be by example and the details will help you
understand what the examples are doing.

Databases

Databases add a great deal of power to what might otherwise be a very ordinary website. In the case of churches, a
website might contain the calendar, articles that are added,
names of the staff or other people or anything else.

A database is a place to hold data. Text files in a directory
or just one text file could be considered a database, but normally we mean a formal relational database when the term is
mentioned.

The exercises in this book use Microsoft® Access™ as the
database of choice. Access™ works well with ASP, it is easy
to understand for beginners as well as the more experienced
and it is a good choice for low traffic websites which is what
church websites tend to be.

Access™ and other relational databases use a language
called SQL or Structured Query Language. SQL specifies
requests for data and can manipulate the data within a relational database. The following is an example of a SQL query
of an Access™ database:

```
SELECT Readings.Reading, Readings.Day
FROM Readings
WHERE (((Readings.Day)=Date()-#1/1/2006#+1));
```

This query retrieves the daily Bible reading for the current day from the database. The first line tells it the type of statement and the fields from which it needs data. The second line tells it which table to use. The third line tells it what conditions must be met for the data to match. In this case the Day of the reading had to match the day of the current date.

The details of what you need to know to build the website example in this book will be given as we move through the steps. Your website may require more or less than is required by the example.

A Lot of Material

A broad range of material has been covered in this step, but the details have been left somewhat sketchy. Don't worry if you don't grasp how to use all of this yet. It is always easier to understand computer languages by doing than by reading about them. If you didn't type the code of the exercises by hand then you should go by and do that. As was stated before, there is something about typing the code, even if someone tells you what to type, that makes it easier to learn how to do the work. The exercises in later steps will continue to ask you to do certain things either as a learning exercise or to move closer to having a complete, working and maintainable website. Doing the work that is asked will help you to develop your website.

Step 6:
Find a Server

Whether you realize it or not, every website that is available on the web, from the one page site that says "under construction" to the big sites that have hundreds of thousands of hits a day, is made available to you through a piece of hardware known as a server. A web server is just a computer with access to the internet and special software that processes requests for data that are stored there. Large websites have many different machines working together to make the site available to the public. Small websites may be just a regular computer sitting in a bedroom in someone's home. Most websites will have servers that fall somewhere between these two extremes.

Three Options

For the church website there are three options that can be considered. There are the homespun web servers, free web space and hosting companies.

The Homespun Web Server

When a large company decides to have a presence on the web it often makes business sense to purchase hardware, as well as hire people to maintain the hardware and configure the web server software. When a web server or a collection of web servers are business critical, any down time can cost the company a lot of money. Even with thousands of users at any given moment, web users expect a website to be responsive. People are beginning to expect that they will click a link and the page will instantly load. If it doesn't load in a few seconds they begin wondering if it is going to load at all

Most churches have a different situation. With the exception, perhaps, of some of the ultra mega churches, churches do not have the financial resources to buy expensive hardware and pay administrators to watch it to make sure that it is operating twenty-four hours a day, seven days a week.. One of the reasons a church might want a website is to be able to make contact with those people who have odd hours and are awake when the rest of us are asleep. It the server goes down then this isn't possible.

For a church, the do it yourself homespun server might be a member's personal computer that is sitting in his home office or bedroom. It might be pastor's or secretary's computer at church. It might be an old computer that someone donated to the church and one of the tech savvy members decided to install some web server software on it. This kind of server can be fun diversion as a hobby and for someone who wants a dirt cheap way of presenting his poetry or something else to the world it fine, but churches need to present a professional appearance to the people who visit their site.

Homespun web servers can be a maintenance nightmare. Virus software has to be kept up to date. A server needs to be backed up regularly. If users are providing input that is stored on the server then it needs to be backed up daily. Computers stop operating on occasion. Someone has to be around to re-boot the machine when needed or to trouble shoot other problems.

Even in a church that has people with the technical ability to put together a functional web server the costs outweigh the benefits. Just because it is "free" doesn't mean that there are not costs associated with it. The value of volunteer labor is often ignored. If doing something pulls too many people away from more mission critical tasks or if people will soon grow tired of doing the work and let it slip then other options should be considered. The homespun web server is such that it will either require the services of several volunteers to provide adequate reliability or something that is less than the best quality will be used. There are always exceptions to the rule, but churches that are trying to put together a website for the first time are probably not those exceptions.

Free Web Space

Some churches have a tendency to spend so much effort looking for a cheap way of doing things that they end up spending more money than they otherwise would have spent. Free web space has the potential of doing this. Free web space is any space that is available on a web server for which the user does not have to pay. Some blog sites charge nothing for a user to have space on their server. The user can post his innermost thoughts and even pictures if he wants. Some people have built very nice websites that are available in this way. Churches also may have the option of making their site available on shared web space that is made available to them through their association or denomination. The church may have to pay some amount as a donation toward the expenses of maintaining the service or it may have to pay nothing at all. The amount of space may range from being quite limited to being quite substantial.

Free web space that is available to the general public often comes with a price. These services may not be backed up, so if the server crashes you may have to completely rebuild your site from the copies you have on your local machine. There may be no guarantee that the service will remain available. Servers can be expensive to operate and operating them for the benefit of people who are not paying can get old quick. The expenses of these businesses are often paid with advertising dollars, so someone using the service may have to put up with ads showing up. The options for designing a site may be limited if free space is used. Blogs, in particular, have a tendency to draw people away from your site to see the sites of other bloggers.

Server space that is provided by an organization that is dedicated to enhancing the work of your church should be considered carefully. Because the organization is interested in seeing churches like your church have a successful website they may be providing a service that is equivalent to some of the more expensive options. They may have many websites on a server rather than a few or just one, so that can cause a problem if they all have good traffic flow to their sites. They may or may not backup their servers. Some of these organizations are just rebranding the same service that is provided by a pay for use company, so you may be receiving the same quality of service as what you would otherwise have for a higher cost.

Free web space may encourage you to create a website that is a subdomain or even just a directory within a domain. This works, but it is better to have your own domain. On the web, your domain is your identity. If you don't have a domain of your own then your identity is wrapped up in that of some other organization. In a church denomination situation this could make a lot of sense because the structure of the web server could match the organization of the denomination, but in other cases it is not as good.

Having one's own domain has many benefits that are well worth the additional expense. Having a domain name that is tied to the site makes it possible to move the site to a different server without the people who visit the site knowing that a

Unique Domain vs. Shared Domain

Some companies give free web space by parceling out directories so the website might be located at:

```
http:\\www.shareddomainname.com\~username\
```

Some companies share the domain by providing subdomains like:

```
http:\\username.shareddomainname.com\
```

Ideally you want something like:

```
http:\\www.mydomainname.com\
```

change has taken place. E-mail address are connected to the domain name, so having a domain name that will not change makes it possible to have e-mail addresses that will not change no matter how many times the person changes internet service providers. The domain name can be descriptive of your church, so it is easier to find and easier to remember.

There are a few benefits, other than price, that free web space offers that an independent website lacks. The website of where the space is located can sometimes increase the traffic flow to the smaller websites that it is hosting. For this to be useful the other sites that are hosted in the same area need to be of a nature that their visitors are the kind of visitors that you want to visit your site. Even though churches generally believe that everyone is welcome, it does little good to have someone visit your site if they are looking a blog style site and all you have to offer is the times your church will be meeting. It does little good if someone from another city visits looking for a church in their own city instead of yours. These visitors will quickly conclude that you have nothing to offer them and they will quickly move on to another site.

Using a Hosting Company

Hosting companies offer, usually reasonably priced, pay as you go plans. The company owns or leases a bank of servers and for a price they will provide space for your site on one of these servers. The company is responsible for maintaining the servers, upgrading the software, performing the daily backups (if they offer this feature) and you simply provide the website and the domain name.

Shared vs. Dedicated Server

One of the options that hosting companies often offer is the choice between a shared and a dedicated server. A shared server is one that has several website hosted on it. A dedicated server is one that has only one website hosted on it. Except in cases where the server must do a lot of processing for the website, most people will not notice a difference between the two. Church websites usually do not require a lot of processing at the server.

The big difference that many be people see is in the amount of memory available, the bandwidth available and the price. A website can be hosted on a shared server for about $70 per year and that price goes up into the hundreds of dollar for more memory and bandwidth. Space on dedicated servers is into the thousands of dollars per year. Still, this may be cheap when compared to the cost of paying five fulltime salaries to insure that the church's web server is always up. Hosting companies can split the cost of these five people with the several customers that are using their servers.

Features

Hosting companies often offer features that are either included in the base price or as an add on. Some of these features may be software that a person could add to a home spun server, but hosting companies often offer tech support as well. Tech support may not cost them a whole lot because they have people sitting around waiting for the server to go down anyway.

Other features include control panels, statistics, e-mail addresses, site submission tools, site building tools and others. These things look nice on paper, but some of these are just fluff while others are needed.

You may not need unlimited e-mail addresses, but most churches need several. It is good to have an e-mail address for the church office, the pastor, the individual members of the staff, the webmaster and maybe even some of the other church leaders. Rather than listing personal e-mail addresses on the website, the created e-mail addresses should be used. When a person changes his e-mail address the webmaster doesn't have to search every page to change the old e-mail address. Instead he makes one change.

Control panels are the user interface to the settings of the site. If a control panel was not available then it would have to be done by some other means, so while marketing types like to push control panels for what they are worth, they are really more the rule than an exception.

Choosing a Solution

Determining the Needs

The first thing that you will need to do before you decide which solution is best is to consider your needs. What capabilities does the web server have to have? How much traffic do you expect to have? How much data will be stored on the website and made available to users? How many e-mail addresses do you thing you need? Do you have enough money to lease the server space? What free options are available? What language will the scripts be in that you will be running on the server? What about database support? You will want to be able to use your own domain name. You will also want to have multiple domains on the same account as well as your own sub domains.

The table below show the answers to these questions for the example that runs through this book:

Needs of the Website
   Traffic: 1GB / month
   Storage: 500 MB (files and e-mail)
   E-mail Addresses: 8
   Budget: $100 / year
   Free Options: none
   Languages: ASP
   Database: MS Access
   Domain Names: multiple and sub domains

The needs of your own website may look different than this. You may need more, or you may need less. For many churches, the answers shown here are more than adequate to meet their needs. If you aren't sure, use these figures for now, set your own budget and be aware that if your website has greater needs that you may have to do something different.

ServerGrid (*www.servergrid.com*), the company that is hosting this book's website, (at the time of this writing) has several options for scaling up. The needs presented above fall easily within the provisions of their cheapest plan. If the website needed greater bandwidth or more storage then it would be possible to obtain that without moving the site. It is likely that other companies have similar plan structures.

Finding a Server to Meet the Needs

If you have experience with a company and you are happy with them then you will probably want to stick with that company rather than moving to another option, unless there is a significant difference in price or features that are offer by another company. If you know that a company doesn't have the features that are required then you would be forced to consider other options. Also, anyone who has never dealt with hosting companies in the past is going to be considering many different options. The are a few sites on the web that allow a user to enter the things that are needed from a hosting company and they will return companies that have plans that meet these needs. A couple of these sites are *www.hostsearch.com* and *www.findmyhosting.com*. My experience has been that it is best to jump immediately to the *Advance Search* feature that both of them have and begin entering the data from the server requirements list that was created. Either site will create a list of plans that you can consider.

Even with this list, you must consider the plans carefully. The plans change frequently and the cheapest one is no always the best one. Some of these companies entice customers with low prices and features they don't need only to charge them a lot of money to upgrade to the features they do.

Some of these companies cater to sites that offer adult content. You probably want to make sure that any company you consider is not listed as permitting adult content. If you are going to have to present this to the church or to a committee it could be very embarrassing if someone were to ask if the company permitted adult content and you had to say that yes they did. Churches should have a good reputation and should void companies that favor the evil side of the internet.

Domain Registration

While considering a solution for a server you will also have to consider domain registration. To register a domain you must go to a website that handles domain registration, type a possible domain name into a form and the site will tell you if you can register that name. If you can, then the site will register your domain for a fee. At this time the fee is around $7 per year, but some companies charge more.

Companies that offer web hosting frequently handle domain registration also. There is no reason why you must register your domain through the same company that you are using for hosting, but you must register your domain if you are going to use one. It is strongly recommended that you do so.

Your choice of a server solution has an impact on your decision concerning a domain. If you are leasing space on a shared server then you would expect to register a domain. If you have a website on a local machine you will also need a domain. If you only have a sub-domain or a folder within someone else's domain then registering a domain will do you no good.

You can find a domain registration company by typing "domain registration" into a search engine. Several results will come up. Evaluate them as you would any other company that you might consider. Look for reviews by customers on other websites. Compare the prices. Read the details of the service they offer. Then pick one and register your domain.

The domain registration company will give you an account and you will have to point the domain at the server once you have space on a server. The company providing the server will provide the needed information and the domain registration company will provide information about how to do this. Usually it requires copying a value from an e-mail sent by the host company into a form on the domain registration company's website.

When you are choosing a domain name you may have to go through several choices before you find something that works well. Since this will be for a church, look for a name that describes the church. Consider using the church's full name or the first letter of each word. If you plan on getting only one domain then get the *org* domain since it is a church, but you might consider registering the *com* and *net* domains as well so that other people don't take them and use them for some other purpose. What you do with the extra domains is up to you. You can point them to one site or create other sites that make use of them.

If you find a domain name you like then go ahead and register it for a year even if you haven't gotten the go ahead from the church. This might cost you a little out of pocket, but it beats having to do another search because someone else liked the name also.

Putting It Off

Signing up for a plan that will give you space on a server can wait a while longer if you are waiting on approval. Even without a server you can design the pages and present then in a way that your pastor, the committee or the church can see what you have planned, but sometimes you need to know what you can do with the server before you get too far because the capabilities of the server will determine part of what you must do to implement the website. Servers do not have a common set of CGI programs or preprocessors, so what you can do on one server may be different from another.

If you are uncertain of the funding, put off beginning to pay for server space for as long as you can. If you sign up for a long period of time and discover that you can't do what you thought you could then you may be out the money you spent. You can do the detailed design and some of the implementation without being able to run ASP or ASP.NET. It doesn't take long to setup a server account, so there is time to wait if you need it. You will need to have access to a web server, though not necessarily the web server where the site will be located, by the time you begin using code for server side scripts.

Step 7:
Do Detailed Design

Moreover I said unto the king, If it please the king, let letters be given me to the governors beyond the river, that they may convey me over till I come into Judah; and a letter unto Asaph the keeper of the king's forest, that he may give me timber to make beams for the gates of the palace which appertained to the house, and for the wall of the city, and for the house that I shall enter into. And the king granted me, according to the good hand of my God upon me.
— Nehemiah 2: 7, 8

In reading the book of Nehemiah, one of the interesting things that one finds is that after Nehemiah caught the vision to rebuild the wall and he had gotten permission from the king to go and do the work he asked the king for letters. These letters were proof that Nehemiah was acting on orders from the king. He used the letters to obtain the material, such as lumber for the gates, that he needed. When Nehemiah reached the Jerusalem he waited a few days and went around the city to look at the wall alone. It was only after he had done this that he went to the people living there and told them of his mission, but when he did he was prepared to tell them what he needed each group of people to do. Nehemiah knew that success requires detailed planning.

Building a website is very different from building a wall. A website usually requires fewer people to build it than a wall. Still, to be successful at building a website one needs to know what he is building. There is a temptation to just begin coding at this point since the server is now just waiting for a website other than the default. There is also that drawing that was done laying out the website. A person might take that and start coding. There is little desire to create a lengthy document explaining the inputs and outputs of everything prior to beginning to code.

Detailed design for a church website doesn't have to be quite as detailed as what is needed for something like a bank's website, for example, that deals with people's life savings on a daily basis. Church websites are usually simple enough that designing and coding can be somewhat combined.

Even though this is true, we will draw a line between design and coding. The layout of the website should be done in the design phase. This design might be done with a drawing program, in XHTML or something else, but it needs to be done before starting to implementation. Also there needs to be a plan of how the different pieces of the site will interact. Determining this plan is part of the detailed design, as well. When it comes time for implementation it is just a matter of doing what we decided needed to be done.

In reality, there is often a play between design and implementation. The design drives the implementation, but constraints that are discovered during implementation feed back into the design. This feedback goes on throughout the life of the website. So let's get started.

Designing the Layout

We already have some idea of how we want the site to look from previous design work that we did. Get the paper on which you drew your sketch of the layout and take a look at it. The one shown here has four areas of content, the header, the navigation bar, the main text and the footer. It also has a picture that crosses one of the lines. For now, this will be treated as a fifth area of content.

As you may recall from what you know of XHTML, these five areas of content can be defined as divisions using the **<div></div>** tag. *Exercise 6* will make use of this fact and help you to create the framework that you will be using to hold the content of your website.

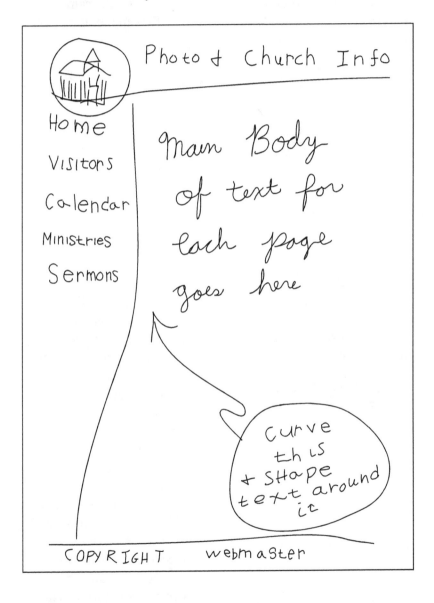

Exercise 6: Designing the Layout

As you did with *exercise 5*, create a new folder to hold the files that you will be creating. This exercise will call for a *design.html* file, a *style.css* file and some image files.

Begin by creating the *design.html* file using the same process you have used to create the text files in the other exercises. Start with it looking like this:

```
<?xml version="1.0" encoding="utf-8" ?>
<!DOCTYPE html PUBLIC "-//W3C//DTD XHTML 1.1//EN"
    "http://www.w3.org/TR/xhtml11/DTD/xhtml11.dtd">
<html>
      <head>
              <title>Church Website Design-Exercise 6</title>
              <meta content="Church Website Design: A step by
step approach - Exercise 6" name="description" />
              <link rel="StyleSheet" href="style.css"
type="text/css" />
      </head>
      <body>
      </body>
</html>
```

Draw the Design

In order to get a good idea of what the website will look like, sometimes it is good to draw picture. Use a graphics program to sketch out the design. Use the actual images and the font type and size that you want to use. It is much easier  to see the result when playing with a graphics tool rather than a text editor. A couple of tools that I have found useful are *The Gimp* and *Xara Extreme. The Gimp* is a free raster graphics tool that can be found on the GNU website. It is very similar to *Photoshop. Xara Extreme* is a reasonably priced vector graphics tool. If you are going to be using graphics on your site then you will need at least one of these or some other quality graphics tool.

When determining the size of image you should create, assume that the user has a browser screen width of 770 pixels for displaying a website. Many people may have more than this and some may have less, but this number is enough for a browser with a six pixel border and a ten pixel scroll bar to display the full width of your site without the need for a horizontal scrollbar. If a page must scroll it is better for it to scroll up and down and not left and right. Users expect to have to scroll down but become frustrated when a website requires them to scroll from left to right. The 770 pixels is based on an assumption of a 600x800 pixel screen.

Always use layers when creating an image that will be used for design purposes. You will probably want to go back to move things around and you might even want to use some of the layers as images for your website. This can be difficult if the image contains text that is part of the content.

Be creative with your drawings. If you are an artist then this is your time to shine. If you aren't an artist then find someone who is and put them to work. Most churches have at least one and sometimes several. The important thing here is to produce an attractive design that meets the needs that have been determined for the website and highlights the most attractive features of the church and property.

Start with the pencil drawing design that was created earlier. Follow it, but don't assume that you must follow it exactly. The image on the previous page is based on the line drawing that was created in a previous step. It has some similarities but differences as well. It has the four different text areas plus a placeholder for the image. But some of its lines are not even as straight as the curved lines that appear in the pencil drawing. As long as there is space to say what needs to be said then anything goes.

After a few more iterations the design looks different again. The image that is shown on the next page is a representation of how the website should appear once it is complete. Notice how it makes use of everything we said should

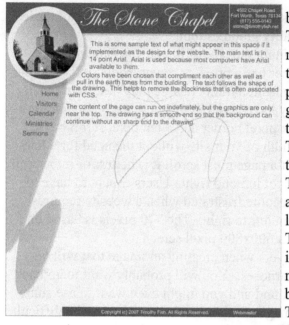

be in the design. There an information bar across the top of the page. The navigation bar is on the left side. There is text in the main area. There is an image in the upper left corner. There is a line of important information at the bottom. The design is different from what many sites have because the text flows around the curved lines that mark the image and the navigation bar. The design has a drop shadow that will cause us to have to do more work, but the improvement in the appearance is well worth the extra effort. The text of the title also creates a problem because the font may not be available on all web clients.

Choosing Colors

The colors that were chosen for the example website are shades of brown. If you go to the website (*http://thestonechapel.timothyfish.net*)and look at the colors used you will notice that the design looks very different in full color than it does on the printed page. There is a significant difference in the impact of grayscale images that are available on the printed page and the images that are available within most web browsers.

The Affect of Color

Color has a way of influencing the emotions without a person even being aware of it. If you think about how color is affecting you then you may not notice it, but psychologists who have studied color and its affects tell us that it affects us more than we realize.

In comparing the color image that is on the website and the grayscale image that you see here, you may notice that the brown image has a friendlier feel to it while the grayscale image is more distant or removed. Some of the sources that refer to such things state that gray implies a solid, timelessness

Colors and What They Say

Black—authority and power, submission to God or man, villain, evil, grieving, neutral

White—purity, clean, safety, neutral

Gray—practical, middle-of-the-road, conservative, old age, neutral

Red—excitement, energy, anger, elevated pulse, color of love, Christmas, always stands out, warm

Blue—favorite color, sky, water, peaceful, tranquil, cold, promotes productivity, the worker's color

Green—nature, money, calm, conservative, wealth, cool

Yellow—cheerful, inflames tempers, difficult to view, concentration, cowardice, very warm

Orange—energetic, flamboyant, fun, happy, sunrise, sunset

Purple—royal, luxury, prosperity

Brown—reliability, solid, stable, friendship, genuine, sometimes sad

that is a kind of middle-of-the-road view while brown may imply friendship as well as stability.

There are some things that churches would like to get across to the users of their website before the user even has a chance to read the content. A church might want to give the impression that it is a relaxing place to be after spending a week in a hectic world. Green is a color that might be used to do this because many people feel more relaxed when they see green. Blue might also be used because of its calming affect. A church might use red to get people excited about something. The use of primary colors together seems to imply an element of fun because there is something childlike in using this combination of colors.

Combining Colors

There is more to color choice than just selecting some colors and throwing them on the website. Some people create websites that seem to be a random mix of colors. Some sites have a black background with nearly every bright color tone that is available thrown across the screen. There seems to be no purpose for the use of color except to get the user's attention. This use of color gives the impression that the site owner's thoughts are just as random as the appearance of the site. For a church, this is not a desirable affect.

Choosing the colors that work well together on a website is a little like choosing the notes that sound good together in a musical chord. There are a few schemes that fairly consistently produce a set of colors that work well together, but mostly it is about what you, those giving you are artistic advice and other stake holders in the website think looks best.

The example for *The Stone Chapel* uses a *monochromatic* color scheme. In this scheme a base color, like brown, is chosen and the other colors have varying levels of brightness but the color is the same. If one color is blue then all the colors will be blue. There might be navy blue, royal blue, sky blue and baby blue, but all of the colors must be blue to be considered monochromatic.

A website with a *monochromatic* color scheme has a consistent feel to it. It also helps to make things that don't fit the scheme stand out. The full color picture in the example catches the viewers attention because it doesn't fit the normal scheme. The lack of conflict within the choice of colors also gives the page a calming affect.

Another common scheme is the *complimentary* color scheme. This scheme is a two color scheme that uses colors directly opposite each other on the color wheel. Orange would be combined with blue, red with green, yellow with purple and so forth.

Using the brown from the example as a base color, a bluish color would be added to the website if the *complimentary* scheme were used. This might cause the site to have a colder feeling to it than what it has with the *monochromatic* scheme. On the other hand, a site that has a base color of blue might be warmed some by added its compliment, which would be a yellowish hue.

There are a number of three hue color schemes. Some of these include the *analogous* color scheme, the *split complementary* color scheme and the *triadic* color scheme. The *analogous* color scheme selects adjacent colors on the color wheel. A website about sea animals might choose this scheme and create a site with the colors blue, blue-green and green in order to mimic the colors of the sea. The *analogous* color scheme has a richness to it that is not found in the *monochromatic* scheme.

Colour Scheme Chooser

On the book website is a feed to a color selection tool that was put together by Mark Rayner of SiteProCentral.com. This color section tool is an interactive tool that will allow you to experiment with all of the selection schemes that are mentioned in this book. Once you have found the colors that you like, you can use the HEX codes that are shown in the tool to build your style sheets.

The *split complementary* color scheme is like combining the *complimentary* and the *analogous* schemes. A base color is chosen on one side of the color wheel and then colors that are analogous to the compliment are chosen. This scheme provides strong contrast but the differences are not as pronounced as in the *complementary* scheme. It can be difficult to get a good balance with this scheme.

The *triadic* color scheme uses colors that are spaced 120° apart on the color wheel. If one of the colors is a primary color then the other two will be primary colors. If one is a secondary color then the other two will be as well.

The *double complementary* or *tetradic* color scheme is formed by selecting a tetrad (four way) of colors. This is done by placing a rectangle on the color wheel. Each color of the four colors has a compliment that is also in the scheme.

No matter what color scheme you use or whether you just pick some colors that you think might look good together there is always an issue of balance. Usually, emphasis should be placed on one color and the others should play secondary roles. In a *complimentary* color scheme, blue might be chosen along with orange. The blue might be used as a background, but using orange as the color for the text might not look good because it raised the importance of the orange hue to the same level as the blue. A better approach would be to use plenty of blue and only use orange for accents. The text might be a shade of blue or black or white could be used.

Black and white are neutral colors, so they can be used with any of the colors that are chosen. A nice look can be obtained by using black or white as the background of the site and then the colors that are chosen using a scheme can be added to this base.

Breaking the Design Apart

Once we have a drawing to work with, the next thing that must be done is to find a way to display the drawing to the user in a way that it looks like what you have in mind. Rather than just displaying the image to the user, it is necessary to convert it into a mixture of images and CSS formatted divisions. CSS was never intended to be used for drawing pictures. It is limited to simple things like rectangles and text. Even the text is limited because the font has to be available on the user's machine or passed to the user's machine. If it isn't available then the browser will use one that is. Sometimes this produces undesirable results.

Start With XHTML and CSS

Always start with what can be handled with XHTML and CSS. XHTML and CSS download faster than raster images and using them reduces the amount of maintenance that will have to be done later.

Starting at the top of the example, the header looks like it might be a candidate for CSS, but it has some problems. One problem is that it uses a font that some users may not have. That means that the church name will have to be passed to the user as an image or the font will have to be changed. Another problem is that it has a shadow. CSS doesn't have shadows like the one that was used in the drawing. It might be done with a PNG file, but some browsers do not support all of the features of a PNG file, so it is better to use other methods. An image is in the top left corner, so it will have to be displayed as an image and not as part something else. The navigation column has a non-straight shape, so it can't be replaced by CSS. The address box at the top can be done with CSS. The main text area can be done with CSS, except it has a squiggly line that cannot be done with CSS. The navigation links can be done with CSS. The copyright notice can be done with CSS.

Make these determinations for your own website drawing then go back to the drawing and remove anything that can be done as CSS and save these rest as a new file. The example file looks like this:

Everything here, with the exception of most of the background, must be displayed as an image. The need to display so much graphical data as just the background of the site can be a major show stopper for some users. A background like this could take as much as fifteen seconds to load for some users. Few people really want to sit around waiting for fifteen seconds while an image file loads and makes the website look attractive. Many people have made decisions to spend hundreds or thousands of dollars in less than fifteen seconds. A user that is waiting fifteen seconds for a page to load may just make the decision that it isn't worth it.

Optimize For Speed

One way to allow the website to keep the look that was intended by the artist and reduce the load time is to remove unnecessary data. The top bar can be reduced to a horizontally repeating image with another image of the text in front of it. The side bar can be sliced into more than one image. The squiggly line can be displayed as one image or if performance is a major issue it can be sliced into additional images so less of the background is included in the image.

Because this is an example, I will not complicate it by completely optimizing the load times. I do, however, recommend that you do so for your own website. Use compression settings that reduce the file size as much as possible without effecting image quality. Slice and dice the images to reduce the need for graphics. In some cases, it is best to redesign to reduce the bandwidth required to view the site.

Cut The Images Into Segments

The image shown here shows the general areas that need to be sliced out of the image and treated as images by XHTML and CSS. Some of these rectangles overlap. In the areas where they do it is necessary to take special care in order to get the site to function properly.

The text at the top appears to be centered and we would expect it to remain centered if the user resizes the window or the user has a screen that is wider than 800 pixels. Getting this to work will require making use of the layers that the image has so that we can extract an image of the text without including any part of the circle and an image of the circle with its shadow without any of the text.

The side bar and the squiggle are both ok as they are, so we can get an image from them easily. The only other image we will need is one that can be used to reproduce the top bar. The image only needs to be one pixel wide.

For your own website, make similar determinations and create images from the master file that match what you determine. The cuts must be exact. If two images are supposed to be joined then make sure that all pixels are included and no pixels overlap between the two images.

The pictures below are the images that were made for the example. You should have something similar for your own development effort.

Build the XHTML and CSS Files

With the images created, the first thing that needs to be done is to remove the default margin that some browsers have. If it is left in place the images will not display correctly. In *style.css*, add the following CSS code:

```
html, body { /* remove the padding and margins */
   margin: 0;
   padding: 0;
}
```

Next, set the font, the font-size, the background-color and the text color. The following shows how it is done for the example:

```
body{
   font-family:Arial;
   font-size:14pt;
   background-color:#F8E8C6;  /* light brown */
   color:#523700              /* dark brown */
}
```

Use the hexadecimal numbers for your own color scheme as well as the font and size that you want. When using hexadecimal numbers, it is a good practice to make a comment describing the color.

Since some of the colors have been set, it is a good idea to change the hyperlink colors also. An unvisited hyperlink can be displayed as the same color as the normal text with an underline. The visited links can have a complementary color.

```
A:link {text-decoration:underline; color:#523700;}
                           /* dark brown */
A:visited {text-decoration:underline; color:#0D1E99;}
                           /* navy blue */
A:active {text-decoration:underline; color:#523700;}
                           /* dark brown */
A:hover {text-decoration:underline; color:#523700;}
                           /* dark brown */
```

Add the Layout Divisions

There are several layout divisions that need to be added in order to get everything to look proper. Each image will have its own division . Notice how each of the example images are put into place before trying to put the images of your own website into place.

All of the layout divisions for the example are of *class layout* so that they can be recognized as a group. The *id* for each is set to a value that distinguishes them from each other.

The first division to be added is the top bar. The top bar runs the width of the browser window. The image is ninety-seven pixels high and one pixel wide. This small image is repeated along the X axis to give the appearance of a bar with a shadow. To make this division, add a layout division to the body of XHTML document.

```
<div class="Layout" id="TopBar"></div>
```

Add the style to the *style.css* file.

```
.Layout#TopBar
{
        background-color:#523700; /*dark brown */
        background-image:url("TopBar.jpg");
        width:100%;
        height:97px;
        background-repeat:x;
        position:absolute;
        left:0px;
        top:0px;
        z-index:1;
}
```

The code sets the background color to the same shade of dark brown that is in the image. This is the prominent color in the image, so if the image fails to load, for some reason, the webpage will still look similar to the way it was intended, but it will have a lower quality.

Setting the background image requires a modifier, *url()*, that lets the system know that the string is an URL rather than ordinary text. Using a relative path will work here, but when scaling this up to a functioning website it would be better to have the full path to the file.

The width tells the browser that the division extends from the left to the right edge. The height matches the height of the image. The background repeat is set to go from left to right. The position is set to *absolute* because the bar must always begin at the top-left position of the webpage.

The *z-index* is set to one because the top bar goes behind nearly everything else on the page. The *z-index* is an arbitrary number that tells where an item is among the layers of over-lapping items on the page. The top bar will be under the pic-ture of the chapel, the text image and the church information box. These divisions will have a higher *z-index*.

Add another division for the circle with the chapel in it. The division has the same code in the XHTML file as the previous division except the *id* is different.

```
<div class="Layout" id="Circle"></div>
```

The style sheet rule is also very similar, but the circle does not repeat and the *z-index* is set so that it is in front of the top bar. Also, the background color is set to the mid tone brown of the sidebar.

```
.Layout#Circle
{
        background-color:#C9A358;  /*mid brown */
        background-image:url("Circle.jpg");
        width:235px;
        height:234px;
        position:absolute;
        left:0px;
        top:0px;
        z-index:5;
}
```

The XHTML code for the side bar is like the other two.

```
<div class="Layout" id="SideBar"></div>
```

The side bar division must begin just below the circle division. The left side is still at zero, but the top must be set. To determine this number you must add the top and the height of the circle. This gives a top position of 234. The z-index of the side bar can be set to five to match the circle, but it really doesn't matter in this case.

```
.Layout#SideBar
{
        background-color:#C9A358;  /*mid brown */
        background-image:url("SideBar.jpg");
        width:175px;
        height:553px;
        position:absolute;
        left:0px;
        top:234px;
        z-index:5;
}
```

The squiggle is a little different because it needs a parent division to put it in the right location. Create another division like the rest.

```
<div class="Layout" id="SquiggleParent">
        <div class="Layout" id="Squiggle"></div>
</div>
```

Unfortunately, the squiggle also presents a problem with some browsers. It can be placed at an absolute location, but it wouldn't look right with a wider screen setting and a centered position is more desirable. Centering is done by setting the left and right margins to auto, but some browsers have a bug that prevents this from working correctly.

There is a third party fix that can be at the web server level so every user will be able to see the page as it should appear even if the user is unaware that his browser doesn't work the way it should, unless the user has disabled the use of JavaScript. The fix is a JavaScript file that was created by David Schontzler and distributed under the Gnu general Public License. The fix is available at *http:// www.stilleye.com/temp/IEmarginFix.zip.* Use it by placing the *IEmarginFix.js* file in the same folder as the HTML file and adding the following to the head block after the style sheet declarations:

```
<script src="IEmarginFix.js" type="text/javascript"></script>
```

With the script in place, write the rules for the two divisions.

```
.Layout#SquiggleParent
{
        position:absolute;
        top:234px;
        right:0px;
        left:175px;
        z-index:0;
}
.Layout#Squiggle
{
        background-color:#F8E8C6; /*light brown */
        background-image:url("Squiggle.jpg");
```

```
    width:357px;
    height:304px;
    margin-left:auto;
    margin-right:auto;
    top:300px;
    z-index:0;
}
```

The title also requires a parent division to center it in its proper location, but it also has need of an **<img/>** tag. The image tag allows alternate text to be placed where an image is if the image does not load. This is also used by text readers for the blind and search engines. Even through the appearance would be the same without the image tag, the alternate text is too important to leave out. The church name is also part of the content of the website, so it should, by convention, be in the XHTML document rather than the CSS file.

```
<div class="Layout" id="TitleParent">
<div class="Layout" id="TitleText"><img src="TitleText.jpg"
alt="The Stone Chapel" /></div>
</div>
```

The style sheet rules are very similar to what has been implemented in the other cases. The *z-index* is two, so that the image will be in front of the top bar. The title text will self center on the screen.

```
.Layout#TitleParent
{
    position:absolute;
    top:0px;
    left:235px;
    right:145px;
    z-index:2;
}
.Layout#TitleText
{
    background-color:#523700; /*dark brown */
    width:392px;
    height:79px;
    margin-left:auto;
    margin-right:auto;
}
```

A 135 pixel space as been left open between the end of the *TitleParent* and the right edge of the screen. This should be just the right amount of space to place the church address, phone number and e-mail. All of these things are content, so they will be placed in the XHTML file.

Only one division with a paragraph to mark the data is required in the XHTML file.

```
<div class="Layout" id="ChurchInfo"><p>4502 Chapel Road<br>
                            Fort Worth, Texas 76134<br>
                            (817) 555-0143<br>
                            <br>
                            stone@timothyfish.net</p>
</div>
```

The style sheet rule is similar to the other rules. The font size is set using pixels rather than points. Depending on the user's machine, text set with points can vary in size in relation to the graphics because the machine assumes a different dots per inch (DPI) count. Using points helps to insure that the box remains a box that fills the area desired.

```
.Layout#ChurchInfo
{
        background-color:#523700; /*dark brown */
        border-color:#F8E8C6; /*light brown */
        border-width:thin;
        border-style:solid;
        color:#F8E8C6; /*light brown */
        width:135px;
        height:76px;
        position:absolute;
        right:0px;
        top:0px;
        text-align:center;
        font-size:12px;
        z-index:10;
}
```

There are five navigation buttons, so five divisions will be required to position the linking text. As shown here, they should be given somewhat generic ids, so that that the content and the presentation continue to stay separate. The names are included in the division. The *NavParent* is an invisible box that sits in front of the side bar image and makes it possible to position the navigation links from the right of the sidebar image. The side bar division could be used for spacing, but the main text division needs to be on a layer that is between the navigation text and the side bar image.

```
<div class="Layout" id="NavParent">
<div class="Layout" id="Nav1"><p>Home</p></div>
<div class="Layout" id="Nav2"><p>Visitors</p></div>
<div class="Layout" id="Nav3"><p>Calendar</p></div>
<div class="Layout" id="Nav4"><p>Ministries</p></div>
<div class="Layout" id="Nav5"><p>Sermons</p></div>
</div>
```

Because the *NavParent* is required to be the same size as the side bar division, a change must be made in how the side bar style sheet rule is declared. The code below splits the original rule into two and applies the positioning (with the exception of the *z-index*) to the *NavParent* as well.

```
.Layout#SideBar, .Layout#NavParent
{
        width:175px;
        height:553px;
        position:absolute;
        left:0px;
        top:234px;
}
.Layout#SideBar
{
        background-color:#C9A358; /*mid brown */
        background-image:url("SideBar.jpg");
        z-index:5;
}
```

Each division has to be positioned so that it follows the curve of the background graphic. The *z-index* should be set to where these divisions are in front. Links will not work if they are behind something. You may have to play with the positioning until you get it where you want it.

```
/* NavParent is a box to hold the navigation links.
it is the same size as the SideBar and shares a rule
with it, above.*/
.Layout#NavParent
{ z-index:10;
}
/* This rule applies to all Navigation Links */
.Layout#Nav1, .Layout#Nav2, .Layout#Nav3, .Layout#Nav4,
.Layout#Nav5
{       position:absolute;
        width:55;
        font-size:20px;
}
/* The individual links. */
.Layout#Nav1
```

```
{        right:30px;
         top:0px;
}
.Layout#Nav2
{        right:35px;
         top:30px;
}
.Layout#Nav3
{        right:45px;
         top:60px;
}
.Layout#Nav4
{        right:50px;
         top:90px;
}
.Layout#Nav5
{        right:60px;
         top:120px;
```

Now all that needs to be done is to add the proper hyper-link to each of the five divisions and the navigation will be finished. The specific links will be determined by the implementation of the site. The *Home* link might look something like the code below and the others will follow the same format.

```
<div class="Layout" id="Nav1">
        <p id="Nav"><a href="design.html">Home</a></p>
</div>
```

Layout the Main Text Area

The main text area is interesting because it also curves around the graphic, but it does it somewhat differently than what was done with the navigation links. It is a style that few websites are using. Part of this may be because the elements in CSS are rectangular and it is easier to create one box to hold the text than to do the work required to put the text in a curve.

Even though the technique is an evolution of a technique many of the early HTML developers stumbled across while trying to get their documents to look right, some people may be unaware that it is possible, or just haven't thought about it. There are so many things that we never figure out how to do because we never thought about trying to do them. The early HTML developers would usually stumble across the technique because they had a problem that needed a solution. We all know that necessity is the mother of invention. New standards and new tools have removed some of the necessity of creative techniques, so the inventiveness of the amateur web developer is not what it once was.

Some people may know the technique, but don't use it because they prefer to have straight lines. Even if someone doesn't like the look that is created by the technique, it is well worth learning because there are many things that can be done using the technique. Anyone who is creating pages for the web needs this technique as a tool in his toolbox.

Background On The Technique

My first real taste of HTML was in 1997. This was also the year that the first HTML standard was released, though one had nothing to do with the other. My only reference was a document I had found on the internet that had been put together by some college student. It listed each of the HTML tags, the purpose of the tag and whether Netscape or Internet Explorer® supported the tag. The fact that I was able to do what I needed to do with only that short document says a great deal about how easy HTML is to use.

One of the things that frustrated me was that things didn't always go where I expected. HTML was intended to describe content and I wanted it to describe the presentation. On hack was to use tables to specify where the images were to be displayed. Another was to use small images as spacers. Many people were doing similar things at the time, so while I discovered the use of spacers for myself, I was neither the first person nor the last person who decided to use spacers made from images.

With wide support of CSS, there is no longer any need to use spacer images, though some people still do. The technique presented here is very much like that technique. In that technique a person who wanted to move text over five pixels would use a small 1x1 image with the **<img>** tag inline with the text. The width of the image would be set to five and the text would be spaced five pixels from what came before it. With CSS there is now the capability to place an image or another element to the left of the right of a paragraph and have the text flow around it. The content doesn't have to be changed with inline image tags for this to happen. The star on the right is an example of something similar in a printed document. The text goes up to the image, but the software  used to typeset this book knows not to place text in the area of the image.

In XHTML and CSS, this is done through the use of float. Below is an XHTML example that displays a blue star to the right of the text. The files are located in the same place as the *Exercise 6* files.

```
DOCTYPE html PUBLIC "-//W3C//DTD XHTML 1.1//EN"
    "http://www.w3.org/TR/xhtml11/DTD/xhtml11.dtd">
<?xml version="1.0" encoding="utf-8" ?>
<html>
<head>
<title>Church Website Design-Exercise 6 Float Right Example
</title>
    <meta content="Church Website Design: A step by step
    approach - Exercise 6 Float Right Example"
    name="description" />
    <style type="text/css">
        .Image#IMG1 { float:right; }
        p {font-size: 24pt;}
    </style>
</head>
<body>
  <div class="Image" id="IMG1"><img alt="Star"
    src="Star.jpg" /></div>
  <p>This is just some text to show what happens with a float
    is used to pull an image out of the flow by floating it
    to the right.  As you can see. The text flows around
    it. To get this to happen the image must be declared with
    a style rule of  float right.</p>
</body>
</html>
```

Another division might be created to float on the other side. The style rule would be:

```
.Image#IMG0 { float:left}
```

The division would be:

```
<div class="Image" id="IMG0"><img alt="Star 0"
src="Star.jpg" /></div>
```

When two images are floated to the same side something
that seems unusual, at first, happens. To illustrate this,
FloatRightExampleII.htm uses two different stars. The code
is as before but with the following differences:

```
.Image#IMG0 { float:right}
.Image#IMG1 { float:right;}

<div class="Image" id="IMG0"><img alt="Star 0"
src="Star.jpg" /></div>
<div class="Image" id="IMG1"><img alt="Star 1"
src="StarII.jpg" /></div>
```

   This causes the
browser to put two stars
side by side on the right
side of the screen.
Given that we weren't
very explicit about
where the stars should be
displayed on the right side, this seems very logical until we
realize that the first star is displayed on the right and the second is on the left. This doesn't seem to match the left to right
reading order that we are used to, so let's take a look at what
is going on.
   According to W3C, elements that are floated are first positioned in the normal flow and then removed from the flow
and pushed over as far as possible in float direction. Because
the first star was the first one the browser encountered while
reading the XHTML in a top to bottom, left to right pattern it
was the first to be repositioned. Nothing in the flow had been
displayed so the normal place for it in the flow is the top left
corner. Starting at that point it was picked up out of the flow
and shoved as far over to the right as it could be. This places
it at the top right corner. The next element in the flow is the
second star. Because the first star is no longer in the way, the
normal position in the flow is once again the top left corner.
It was picked up out of the flow and shoved over, but this

time it can't be shoved all the way over to the right because the first star is already there to block the way. The position of the first is already set and will not be reconsidered. Finally the text is placed in the normal flow. The normal flow flows around floated images that are already in place, so the results are as they should be even though it looks incorrect.

If instead of side by side the desire effect is to have the first box above the second then the *clear* property could be used like below.

```
.Image#IMG0 { float:right; }
.Image#IMG1 { float:right; clear:right}
```

This produces results like is shown with the stars on the right. *Clear* specifies which side cannot have another floated element adjacent to it. By clearing the right side of the second image the browser knows that it should not place the image next to a previously placed image so it moves the new image down until it has room to place the image without interfering with a previously placed element. Once it is below the first image, it can be moved farther over to the right, so the final location is directly below the first.

If CSS were a logical language, there would be no difference between clearing the right side of the second image and clearing the left side of the first image. But, CSS and XHTML are not logical languages. They are interpreted. The browser knows only what it has been told. It doesn't look ahead. If it hasn't reached a line that will tell it not to place something somewhere then it considers that space open. It also does not reconsider. If something is in position it will not be repositioned until the next redraw and the redraw will occur in the same order as before, unless there is a script to tell the browser to do otherwise.

Drawing With Empty Space

The basic technique that is required to shape the main text around the navigation bar is like what was used with the star images, except no images will be used, there are more blocks and the blocks will be smaller. The blocks will be about the same size as the blocks that are drawn on this page, but the blocks on the webpage will be invisible. The main text will be in a normal rectangle, but with the blocks blocking the flow of the document the text will have the appearance of following the curve of the navigation bar.

To accomplish this, division blocks must be placed from the top of the text area to the lowest part of the text area where the text would cover part of the shadow from the navigation bar. We must be careful that none of the shadow gets covered because the lack of a shadow on the text or other elements would look unnatural to the user. The user should have the impression that he text is resting on the background and would slide under the navigation bar if it could be moved.

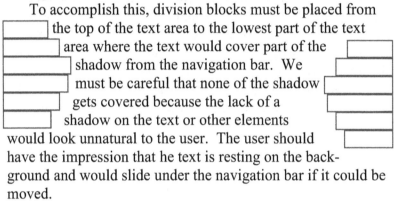

The main text block is the first block to be positioned and is the parent block for the spacers and the document's main text. The top of the text block must be no higher than the bottom of the shadow on the top bar. The left of the block should be no closer to the left edge than we want text to be displayed on the left side. Because the navigation bar terminated nicely, the text can go all the way to the left after flow gets past the bar.

```
<div class="Layout" id="MainText">
<!-- Spacers Go Here -->
<!-- Document text goes here! -->
</div>

/* Main Text Box with spacers */
.Layout#MainText
{
        position:absolute;
        top:97px;
        left:0px;
        width:100%;
```

```
z-index:7;
}
```

   As with everything else that has been presented here, creating the spacers involves modifying the XHTML file and the CSS file. In the XHTML file many divisions must be created. How many must be created depends on how fine tuned the developer wants the positioning to be. For the best accuracy there needs to be one division per pixel height of the image that the text is to follow. That fidelity would require about seven hundred divisions. It is better to settle for something less. Obtaining that fidelity would involve some programming to generate the divisions and the width of each. One division per line of text is adequate, but it may still look a little blocky. Here I am using a division height of one *em* with a font height of twenty pixels. It takes about thirty divisions to cover the image. It is much easier to set the width of thirty elements than to set seven hundred.

   The elements all look similar. They have the following form:

```
<div class="Spacer" id="SpacerL1"></div>
```

   The only thing that changes is the number at the end of the *id*. If Spacers are to be used on both sides then the form should be:

```
<div class="SpacerL" id="SpacerL1"></div>
<div class="SpacerR" id="SpacerR1"></div>
```

   All of the really interesting stuff is in the CSS file, including a commented out *lime* background color. It helps to be able to see where the spacers are and how wide they are. Setting the widths will take a while. Though I set the widths by hand, I used a screenshot from Microsoft® Visual Studio® in The Gimp along with the in information tool so that I could find the number of pixels from the edge of the shadow to the left edge. Visual Studio® displays the edge of the division so it is easy to see where it is compared to the image. The same thing can be done by having the browser draw the borders around the divisions until you have then placed correctly.

```
.Spacer
{
        font-size:20px;  /* Change this number to change the
division height.*/
        height:1em;
        float:left;
        width:10px;
        clear:left;
        /*background-color:lime;*/
}
.Spacer#SpacerL1{ width:225px;  }
.Spacer#SpacerL2{ width:230px;  }
.Spacer#SpacerL3{ width:223px;  }
.Spacer#SpacerL4{ width:218px;  }
.Spacer#SpacerL5{ width:205px;  }
.Spacer#SpacerL6{ width:175px;  }
.Spacer#SpacerL7{ width:172px;  }
.Spacer#SpacerL8{ width:167px;  }
.Spacer#SpacerL9{ width:160px;  }
.Spacer#SpacerL10{ width:158px;  }
.Spacer#SpacerL11{ width:153px;  }
.Spacer#SpacerL12{ width:143px;  }
.Spacer#SpacerL13{ width:137px;  }
.Spacer#SpacerL14{ width:134px;  }
.Spacer#SpacerL15{ width:123px;  }
.Spacer#SpacerL16{ width:113px;  }
.Spacer#SpacerL17{ width:105px;  }
.Spacer#SpacerL18{ width:99px;  }
.Spacer#SpacerL19{ width:155px;  }
.Spacer#SpacerL20{ width:160px;  }
.Spacer#SpacerL21{ width:158px;  }
.Spacer#SpacerL22{ width:158px;  }
.Spacer#SpacerL23{ width:150px;  }
.Spacer#SpacerL24{ width:140px;  }
.Spacer#SpacerL25{ width:136px;  }
.Spacer#SpacerL26{ width:127px;  }
.Spacer#SpacerL27{ width:118px;  }
.Spacer#SpacerL28{ width:105px;  }
.Spacer#SpacerL29{ width:94px;  }
.Spacer#SpacerL30{ width:80px;  }
```

It is well worth it but it takes a lot of work to get this right, when doing it by hand. If you have a tool that will allow you to draw the rectangles over the image and get the width of each spacer it will help you immensely in designing your own church website. Some tools will allow you to use the mouse to set the width of the divisions against a background image. This can be a big help.

The Final Touch

The last thing that must go into the design is the copyright information and the webmaster's email address. The hand drawn design shows this information at the bottom of the page. One way to do this is to make it part of the MainText division. The code to create a simple dark brown division with the copyright information and the webmaster's email address is below:

```
<!-- Footer Goes here -->
<div class="Layout" id="Footer">
<p>Copyright &copy; 2007 Timothy Fish. All Rights Reserved.
          &n
bsp;<a href="mailto:webmaster@timothyfish.net"
id="Footer">webmaster</a></p>
</div>
```

```
/* Footer */
.Layout#Footer
{
        background-color:#523700; /*dark brown */
        color:#F8E8C6; /* light brown */
        font-size:12px;
        width:540px;
        text-align:center;
        z-index:7;
}
A#Footer:link {text-decoration:underline; color:#F8E8C6;}
                               /* light brown */
A#Footer:visited {text-decoration:underline; color:#C9A358;}
                               /*mid brown */
A#Footer:active {text-decoration:underline; color:#F8E8C6;}
                               /* light brown */
A#Footer:hover {text-decoration:underline; color:#F8E8C6;}
                               /* light brown */
```

The anchor tag style had to be modified because the normal colors are the same as the background.

Trying It Out

After doing this much work one likes to see if things are working the way they should. To see how the designed page looks you can add some XHTML code directly following the comment that states, "<!-- Document text goes here! -->." Either write the XHTML yourself or copy it from somewhere.

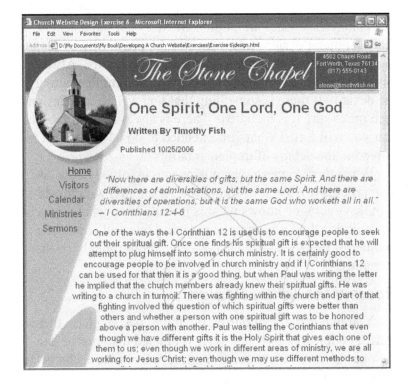

You will want to have several lines so that you can see how the text will flow around the navigation bar.

In terms of having an attractive and functioning website, a person could end the design process at this point, make copies of the XHTML file that has been created, add articles by pasting XHTML code into the same place as the test XHTML code has been pasted, add links with anchor tags on the navigation bar and the individual pages and call it good. Many church webmasters have done this very thing. Many webmasters have also had trouble maintaining their websites, so don't spend too much time admiring your work at this point. There is much more work that needs to be done.

Designing the Content

With the design of the presentation in place it is time to take a more detailed look at the content. Without a detailed design of the content it is difficult to know how to implement the different features in the implementation phase. Since most church websites are implemented by the same person that designed the site there is usually the possibility of designing it on the fly, but doing so can lead to problems. Always design like you aren't going to be the person implementing the design. If there is something that you want in the design then make sure it is included. There is always the possibility that you will forget what you intended to do when you get involved in the details of implementation.

When there is more than one person involved in the design process it is good to communicate enough with the design that everyone knows what is intended and what the website will do when it is complete. Doing this will reduce the number of times you have people say, "but I thought it was going to…"

Review the Initial Design

You may recall that during the initial design phase there were a couple of charts that were produced that looked like the ones below. Before going too far, pull out these charts and review what you intended to do.

Need	Page
Description of Church	Home
Doctrinal Statement	Home
Descriptions of Ministries	Ministries
Calendar	Calendar
Directions	Home
What to expect	Visitors
Contact Info	Home
How to be saved	Visitor
Photos	Home
Sermons	Sermons

We already know that all of the boxes in the drawing will have to have a page associated with it. As some of these are

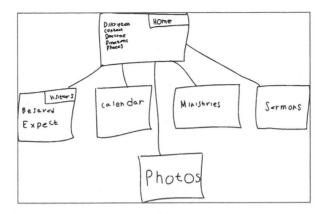

Diskription
Contact
Doctrine
Directions
Photos

Home

Visitors
Be saved
Expect

Calendar

Ministries

Sermons

Photos

implemented there may be additional pages that will be created. The Home page doesn't appear to be a major concern.
The items listed are either links to other pages or articles.
Both of these are easy to create. The Visitors and Ministries
pages are a similar situation. The other three leave us with
some choices that have to be made.

Designing the Calendar

It is one thing to say that you want a church calendar, but
what is it that you really want? Do you want a calendar that
matches the design and layout of the website? Do you have
the time and expertise to create it? Do you want a list of
events? Are you willing to settle for a free calendar that is
hosted on another site and is funded by user clicks? Do you
have the money to pay for a better option?

As long as it is free, it is better to start with less than is
available then consider more costly options later. Free calendars are clearly not the most attractive option with their ban-
ner ads and gaudy color schemes. It isn't really the type of
image that you want to present to visitors, but it is free and
that beats the twenty-five dollar or more annual fee for some
calendars. A custom calendar that fits into the website design
is cheap enough with qualified labor volunteer labor and a
custom calendar can be completely integrated into the site
rather than just being an add on, but it takes time to build one
that meets your needs. Because we have given ourselves a
budget constraint of $100, we are nearly forced to use either

the free external hosted option or to build the calendar. Unless there is some compelling reason to do otherwise it is probably best to take the free route.

By making that decision, the design now should indicate that by calendar we mean that the site links to an another site that hosts the calendar for the church. The decision of which site will be used can either be made at this point or it can be pushed off until later. Sites that offer this service are easy to find by doing an internet search. Even Google has gotten into the act and is offering a calendar service. You will need to decide which company provides a calendar that best fits your situation.

Designing The Sermons Page

The sermons page could be one of many things. It could be several things. The sermons might be transcripts. In this case there might be a need to upload PDF files or to create new web pages. The ability to create new web pages and to upload files is a necessity for a well maintained website, so that is not an issue. The sermons might also be in some audio format. That raises the question of whether the files will be streamed or whether the user must download the file to play it. There are sites that allow sermons to be uploaded to their servers. Some churches make use of this.

The *fortworthbaptistchurch.org* site is designed to upload the sermons to it's server and to play the audio files directly from the sermon web page. There are several advantages to doing it this way, but it requires some programming to get it to work. The main reason it uses this method is because it made it possible to nearly automate the process of uploading sermons. On a weekly basis the church secretary receives a two CDs from the sound technicians that are marked to tell her which track holds the sermon. Using a conversion program she converts the track to an audio file. Then into a password protected form on the church website she types the information about the sermon and selects the audio file to upload. After she submits the form, the file is uploaded and the database is updated to include a link to the new sermon in a list of sermons. There is no need to manually create a link and the website always lists the sermons that are available.

The free upload services have a similar form, but it is harder to provide the user with just the sermons from one church. Also, the church website might contain just a link to the other site, but not to an actual sermon.

The decision of how your website will make sermons available is ultimately yours. One possibility is to try one of the free upload areas for a while to see if it works for you. If it doesn't there is always the option of storing the sermons on your site.

Designing the Photo Page

The photo page is another page that might be outsourced to another site. There are several sites available that want you to put pictures on their servers and that allow you to share these pictures with whomever you please. On the other hand, uploading pictures and providing them to the user from your own site is not that difficult either.

If you are going to do it from your own site then you will probably want a form that will upload the picture for you and provide brief comments that you write. The users would then be able to see the pictures from your site rather than being taken away.

Exercise 7: The Design Review

The design review is a chance for the pastor, the church leaders, even the church as a whole to take a look at the design and make comments. It is also a good opportunity to do some informal usability testing. If a prototype has been created and people are having trouble figuring out what to do or they aren't finding the expected things then there are probably some usability issues that need to be resolved. If the church had paid a company to develop the site then it would be expected that the company would present some kind of plan for the development of the site prior to beginning to write code.

Unfortunately, churches that are relying on volunteer labor seldom see the need to do a design review whether it is formal or informal. It isn't that churches don't care as much as it is that many of the members lack understanding when it comes to technology and how to implement a website.

Often, the webmaster answers to himself. As long as he doesn't do something that gives the pastor or one of the other church leaders a reason to be upset with him, he is on his own except when someone has an idea of something that might be added to the website. Frequently, the webmaster is happy to be completely responsible for his little area of service and he really doesn't want other people telling him that he is doing something wrong. Design reviews are one of those places where it can seem that everyone is saying that something is wrong, so a webmaster may be reluctant to schedule a design review.

In looking at the roles within the web ministry, the responsibility for calling the design review falls within the role of the ministry leader. The pastor of the church is not likely to schedule one because he is too busy with other things to keep up with what is going on with the website. The web ministry doesn't usually fall within another ministry, so there probably isn't anyone other than the web ministry leader or the webmaster who feels the need to call for a review unless the web ministry is doing something for another ministry.

Who Should Be Invited

Anyone can be invited, but the most important people to invite to a design review are the people who are impacted by the design or design changes. If the design includes new features for the Youth Ministry then the youth minister and other people who work with the youth should be given a chance to review the design and make comments. If it is a new website then a blanket invitation to the whole church might be extended.

Preparing For The Design Review

For a successful design review you need to be able to communicate the design to people in a meaningful way so that they understand it and the impact it has on them personally.

By successful I mean to say that people provide useful feedback that allows you to make changes that improve the website. The best way to get useful feedback is to let people explore the design through the use of a prototype, so to be prepared for a design review you will have to have prototype of your website.

Create a folder named *Exercise 7*. Into this folder copy the *design.html* file from *Exercise 6* and also copy the files that are referenced by *design.html*. When you have done this, change the link for *Home* to point to *index.html*. Set the *Visitors* link to *visitors.html*. Set the *Calendar* link to the calendar you plan on using. Set the *Ministries* link to *ministries.html*. Set the *Sermons* link to either *sermons.html* or the site you plan on using for sermons. *Copy design.html* and rename the copy *index.html*. This is one of the common names that is used to the first page of a website.

In the area that is intended for the main text of the *index.html* file, write XHTML code that includes all of the

things that are supposed to be on the home page of the site. Create the other files by making a copy of *design.html* and renaming the copy to the name that is referenced in the *design.html* file.

In each of the files include information and placeholders for all of the information you plan on placing in these when the site is complete. Don't spend a lot of time doing this because it is only so that people will have something to look at. There should be enough that they feel like they are looking at the website, but it is ok to have things like "The link you clicked will play a sermon in the final version." Be sure to update the title and description in the header of each document to state what it is.

So far, the files have been created can be served from a CD without any additional software. Because people who are involved with churches are very busy and meetings are seldom mandatory, it might be best to provide the prototype in a form that people can take home with them and view at their leisure, so burn the folder that contains the prototype to CDs that can be passed out to key people.

Conducting The Design Review

A design review can be either formal or informal. Unless the situation calls for a more formal process, in a church setting it is probably best to try to keep the design review informal. Some suggestions on how to conduct both versions are presented here.

The Formal Review

Formal reviews are most important in situations where the thing being developed is either big, it is mission critical, expensive or lives are at risk. By formalizing the review it is possible to make sure that all of the design is reviewed before it is passed off to the next phase where a person may not realize that the design has a problem and even if they do it may be late enough that it is difficult to make the change.

There are few things that would call for a church to use a formal review for a website, but if it did there are some things you should know. Formal reviews often encompass more of the design than informal reviews. In a formal review the overall structure of the site would be evaluated. The appearance would be evaluated If there was to be code behind the site then the design of the code would be evaluated.

If the church is going to use a formal review, it should be held in a room where the pages of the prototype can be seen by everyone involved. It is not a good idea to have several people huddle around the computer. The software design should also be made available. Page by page the people involved should be shown each part of the design and given a chance to comment on each section. The people who developed the design should be able to explain what they did and why.

The Informal Review

The informal review is not as accurate about catching potential problems, but few church websites need more than an informal review of the design. An informal review can be done by handing someone a CD and asking them to look at the website on it then make comments. An informal review can also be so informal that the reviewers don't even know that they have taken part in a review.

People often ask the church webmaster about the website. Use this opportunity to find out what people really think about it. These people are interested enough to ask, so they might be interested enough to provide some feedback about the design. Show them the new design and let them tell you what they like and dislike about it. Watch them as they play with it some. Take note of where they go and what they do. Ask them what they would like to see added and it there is something they think should be changed.

Handling a Design Defect

One of the things that design reviews do is detect defects in the design.

What a Defect Is

A defect is anything that is wrong with the design. A defect could be caused by anything and any defect that might cause the final product to be implemented incorrectly is a cause for concern.

Some design defects are simple mistakes, like misspellings or drawing a box where there shouldn't be one. Some are caused by a previous defect. When you were determining what you need the website to do, for example, the people you asked may not have told you everything they needed. When they begin to review the design they might realize that it doesn't include something they need. The fact that the design doesn't include it makes it a design defect even though fixing it requires changes to the requirements or need statements as well.

Making The Modification

If there is a design defect that is discovered then it needs to be corrected before you begin implementing your website. Defects have a way of ballooning until they are completely out of control.

The method that was used to create the prototype has an inherent design flaw that is intended to illustrate this point. Suppose that during a design review of The Stone Chapel prototype some people commented on not liking the email address listed as it is in the box at the top right. They suggest, and we agree, that the email address should be placed with the contact information on the home page, but it doesn't look good with the address. Having created the prototype using a method of copying a template and then making modifications, what must be done to make the change?

Because of the method that was used, making the change requires that each file be touched again. Each file must be opened, corrected and saved. There are eight files with the HTML extension in *Exercise 7*. All eight must be modified. That is fairly simple, but imagine how many would have to be modified if a change in the design takes place after several more pages have been added using the same method as before. Some church websites have hundreds of pages that look identical except for the main body of text.

Making a change, no matter how simple, in hundreds of pages is something that no webmaster wants to do. It is the kind of work that is ideally suited for computers, but it takes too long for humans to do it. It is also a task at which humans quickly bore. The result is that, if the computer can't be told to do it, the task won't get done.

The email address is at best a minor design defect, but the lack of a good way to do maintenance on the site is a major defect. The one constant for churches and websites is that things change. A website that is not designed to be changed is one that is doomed to fail.

A Successful Design Review

A successful design review is one in which defects are detected rather than one in which people talk about how great everything looks. By finding that the email address in the top box should be removed and that there is a problem with how the pages are created the review had at least some success.

The email address might be moved in the prototype, but to correct the other problem there will have to be some implementation. The design should be modified to show, if it does not already, that a database will be used to store content and that the design and content will be combined by the web server before it is sent to the user's browser.

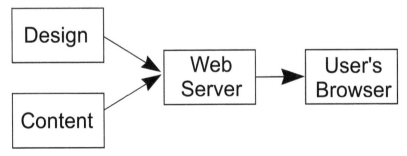

After correcting the design you can declare yourself finished with the design (for this spiral) and move on to the next step.

Step 8:
Develop The Code

Even so faith, if it hath not works, is dead, being alone. Yea, a man may say, Thou hast faith, and I have works: shew me thy faith without thy works, and I will shew thee my faith by my works.

– James 2: 17, 18

A good design is like faith. Unless it is put into practice it is useless. Once the design is complete it is time to begin coding. The programming language that we will be using is ASP.

Exercise seven demonstrated that a website could be created with XHTML and CSS, but it also demonstrated that maintaining such a website is a major problem if content is added frequently or in large amounts. At the end of the step seven a design was presented that called for the server to combine the presentation with the content prior to providing the information to the user. There are several ways to do this. The one presented here utilizes the prototype that was created in the previous step along with ASP and an Access database.

Don't Panic!

If you have never written code and you are unsure how to make use of Access, don't panic. The coding that is required at this point is fairly simple and most of it you can copy from the code presented here with a few modifications and have a easily maintainable website. That is provided you comply with the license and do not violate my copyright. In other words, you are welcome to use it for a church website as long as you own a copy of this book and give me proper credit. All other uses are prohibited without permission. Others may want to build on the code presented here and develop even better sites from it. The modifications that are required are explained in detail and after making them you will be better prepared for learning more about how to develop and maintain websites.

Setting Up The Environment

To develop a website you will need a development environment as well as server space. Some people like to have a web server running on their local machine as part of the development environment, even if they plan for the site to be hosted on another machine. This can be a nice feature, but some operating systems make this difficult and it is not absolutely necessary, so the assumption here is that you do not have a server on your machine.

The Local Machine

You will need a folder on you machine to hold the website. For now, call it *Exercise8*. Anything that you place in this folder will be moved to the server when you are ready to do so. This folder should be an exact match of what is on the server.

The Web Server

If you haven't signed up for access to a server, you will need to do so before you can proceed. My website is hosted by *ServerGrid*. You may have to do things slightly different than what is explained here if you go with another company. Your hosting company should be able to help you if you need it.

The hosting company will provide you with the information about the location of the server. This information must be provided to the domain registration company. This is usually done by filling out a form that is tied to your account with the domain registration company. You will also need to tell the hosting company what domains you have. In my case, this is through the *ServerGrid Control Panel*. To add a domain there is a link that is appropriately named "Domains." This goes to a page showing all of my domains and it has an option to add a domain. This goes to a page where it is possible to register a domain, have *ServerGrid* host a website currently hosted by someone else (or registered through another company), or add a subdomain (third level domain) to one of their domains. Your hosting company should have something similar and should be able to help you through the process.

Even after you have setup your accounts with the hosting company and the registration company, you may not be able to type *www.mydomainname.org* into a server and see your site. It takes a while for the information to make its way to the various nodes of the internet. Your hosting company may give you an alternate access method until this happens.

After this a few days you should be able to access the site through FTP as well as through the hosting company's control panel, if they have one. For the purpose of this example, I have created a subdomain *thestonechapel.timothyfish.net*. One way I can gain access to this is by going to Internet Explorer® and in the place for the URL typing "*ftp:\\thestonechapel.timothyfish.net*." After entering the user id and password for my web server account I can see several folders showing the various domains that are defined for that account. One of these is "*thestonechapel.timothyfish.net*." From this point forward, Internet Explorer® works similarly to the way Windows® Explorer normally does.

Opening the "*thestonechapel.timothyfish.net*" folder shows me the contents. One of the files is "index.html" which is the default file that is used when a new domain is setup. There are some other files. There is a "cgi-bin" folder that will be used. The rest will be replaced during the process of developing the website.

Copy the *cgi-bin* folder to the development folder on your local machine. Delete the other files and folders, on the server, unless there is some reason why you want to keep them or your hosting company has told you not to delete them. Your development folder and the web server should now be identical.

For *ServerGrid* and other similar servers, the process could have been done through the control panel. Your own situation and preference will determine when you use the control panel and when you use FTP.

Exercise 8: An ASP Application

Exercise 8 covers the process of making the website available to the public. The end result of this exercise is a functioning website that is available at every computer connected to the internet.

Setup

In the same location as the other exercises create another folder and name it *Exercise 8*. Copy the following files from *Exercise 7*.

- Style.css
- Design.html
- Circle.jpg
- SideBar.jpg
- Squiggle.jpg
- Title.Text.jpg
- TopBar.jpg
- IEmarginFix.js

Make the following changes to *design.html*:

Replace,

```
<title>Church Website Design-Exercise 7</title>
<meta content="Church Website Design: A step by step approach
- Exercise 7" name="description" />
```

With,

```
<!-- WARNING: Do not change the next line! of template. -->
<!----- Title and description go here! ----->
```

Replace,

```
<!-- Document text goes here! -->
```

With,

```
<!-- WARNING: Do not change the next line! of template. -->
<!----- Document text goes here! ----->
```

With these changes it will be possible to use the template that we were making copies of in *Exercise 7* as a template for the server to use. The advantage to this is that the theme for a site can be designed using and XHTML file, a CSS file and some image files then when a change needs to take place only the files that define the theme need to be changed rather than changing every file that was derived from those files.

The Page.ASP File

Create a new text file and name it "*page.asp.*" Type the following code into this file:

```
<%'Reads a template, outputs everything but replaces the ti-
tle, description and main text.
  'Copyright (c) 2007 Timothy Fish. All Rights Reserved.


strPathInfo = Request.ServerVariables("PATH_INFO")
Set FileSys=Server.CreateObject("Scripting.FileSystemObject")
Set TStream=FileSys.OpenTextFile
("C:\hshome\tdfish\thestonechapel.timothyfish.net\design.html"
, 1)

DO WHILE TStream.AtEndOfStream <> True
      Line = TStream.ReadLine()
      IF InStr(1, Line,"<!----- Title and description go
here! ----->",vbTextCompare) <> 0  THEN
            Response.Write("<title>Church Website Design-
Exercise 8</title>"&vbCRLF)
            Response.Write("<meta content=""Church Website
Design: A step by step approach - Exercise 8""
name=""description"" />"&vbCRLF)
      ELSEIF InStr(1, Line, "<!----- Document text goes here!
----->") <> 0 THEN
            Response.Write("<h1>This is the test document
text.</h1>"&vbCRLF)
      ELSE
            Response.Write(Line&vbCRLF)
      END IF
LOOP
TStream.Close
%>
```

*Please note that the <u>underlines</u> and **bold text** are not part of the code but are shown here for clarity.*

This code begins with **<%** and ends with **%>**. These symbols are special tags that tell the ASP preprocessor that the information contained between them should be interpreted as ASP rather than XHTML. The code is executed and only those things that are passed to the **Response.Write** functions are included in the XHTML stream that is passed to the browser.

The code opens the file that is underlined to be read as a text stream. To make this code to work for you, change this pathname to reflect your own environment. You will notice that it is not a URL but a full path. See the note on "Getting the Full Path of a Server File" to how to obtain this information.

The ASP code goes into a loop in which it reads each line of the *design.html* file. Each line is passed to the user's browser except for the lines that contain the comments that are shown in bold within the code for the *page.asp* file. Instead of passing these, a different title and description are passed for one of them and for the other a different main body is passed.

To try this new file, copy *page.asp* to the top level domain folder on the server.

Calling *"http://www.mydomainname.org/page.asp"* will give a result similar to the screen shot shown on the next page.

While this is not impressive, by itself, the ability to read a template and replace portions of it with text dynamically

---

Getting the Full Path to a Server File

Some ASP functions require the full server path rather than a relative path or a URL. To get this path, get an ASP file called "GetFullPath.asp" in the location on the server where you want to know the path. This file should have the following code in it:

```
<%@ Language=VBScript %>
<html>
<head>
</head>
<body>
<%
strPathInfo = Request.ServerVariables("PATH_INFO")
Response.Write("<p>"&Server.MapPath(strPathInfo)&"</
p>"&vbCRLF)
%>
</body>
</html>
```

If this is located in the main folder on the server, "http:\\www.mydomainname.org\GetFullPath.asp" will return the path to GetFullPath.asp.

opens the door to allow the real content of the site to be stored separately from the XHTML. The *page.asp* file serves as the starting point for bigger and better things.

A New Index

In *Exercise 7* we created an *index.html* file. It was created in the same way as all of the others by copying *design.html* and renaming it. If *design.html* is to be our definitive design description, *index.html* will have to the first to be changed to support this new concept.

Pointing the Server at an Index

The new index file will be called *index.asp*. The index file is normally the default document for the directory that contains it. If a user specifies a directory on the server without specifying a file we expect the server to show something other than an error message. The default document is what the server shows, but initial setup of a website usually sets either *index.htm* or *index.html* as the default document. We need to set *index.asp* as the default document because *index.html* will no longer exist.

Your server and hosting company will have its own proce-
dure, but it will be similar to *ServerGrid's*. For *ServerGrid*,
one must go to the control panel and select *Web Options*. After that the icon for *Edit Hosting Parameters* must be selected. One of the options on the next screen is *Directory In-
dexes*. If it is off it is necessary to enable it. If it is on then
one must configure it and set *index.asp* as the index. Now
when *index.asp* is uploaded to the server the domain name
will lead directly to it.

Creating Index.ASP

In a similar way to the way *index.html* was created, create
index.asp by copying *page.asp* and renaming it. In the new
file, replace,

```
Response.Write("<title>Church Website Design-Exercise 8</
title>"&vbCRLF)
Response.Write("<meta content=""Church Website Design: A step
by step approach - Exercise 8"" name=""description"" /
>"&vbCRLF)
```

With,

```
%>
<title>The Stone Chapel</title>
<meta content="Church Website Design: A step by step approach
- Home Page" name="description" />
<%
```

Replace,

```
Response.Write("<h1>This is the test document text.</
h1>"&vbCRLF)
```

With,

Everything between the comment "The Document Text
Goes Here!" and the comment "Footer Goes here" from the
index.html file.

Please Note: Visual Basic and vbScript do not allow line-
feeds in strings and functions, so anything that is placed in a
Response.Write statement should be placed on one line even
though this text is forced to show it on multiple lines due to

space constraints. If in doubt, check the examples that are available online.

The *index.asp* file should look like the code beginning on the next page.

```asp
<%'Reads a template, outputs everything but replaces the title, description and main text.
'Copyright (c) 2007 Timothy Fish. All Rights Reserved.

strPathInfo = Request.ServerVariables("PATH_INFO")
Set FileSys=Server.CreateObject("Scripting.FileSystemObject")
Set TStream=FileSys.OpenTextFile("C:\hshome\tdfish\thestonechapel.timothyfish.net\design.html", 1)

DO WHILE TStream.AtEndOfStream <> True
    Line = TStream.ReadLine()
    IF InStr(1, Line,"<!----- Title and description go here! ---->",vbTextCompare) <> 0  THEN%>
        <title>The Stone Chapel</title>
        <meta content="Church Website Design: A step by step approach - Home Page" name="description" />
    <%ELSEIF InStr(1, Line, "<!----- Document text goes here! ---->") <> 0 THEN%>
        <div>
        <h1>Welcome to The Stone Chapel</h1>
        <p>The Stone Chapel is a fictitious small community of Bible believing Christians.
        We have been existence since...well never, actually. Our whole purpose for
        existing is to serve as an example of how to build a church website in the book <i>Church
        Website Design: A step by step approach</i>. Our building isn't even used
        as a church building. It is actually a funeral chapel. If it wasn't for that we
        would ask you to join us at one of the following times:</p>

        <table id="Table1" cellspacing="1" cellpadding="1" width="300" border="1">
        <tr>
        <td style="white-space:nowrap">Sunday School</td>
        <td style="white-space:nowrap">10:00 AM</td>
        <td>Sunday</td>
        </tr>
        <tr>
        <td>Worship</td>
        <td style="white-space:nowrap">11:00 AM</td>
        <td>Sunday</td>
```

```
        </tr>
        <tr>
        <td style="white-space:nowrap">Evening Worship</td>
        <td style="white-space:nowrap">6:00 PM</td>
        <td>Sunday</td>
        </tr>
        <tr>
        <td>Awana</td>
        <td style="white-space:nowrap">6:30 PM</td>
        <td>Wednesday</td>
        </tr>
        <tr>
        <td style="white-space:nowrap">Prayer Meeting</td>
        <td style="white-space:nowrap">7:00 PM</td>
        <td>Wednesday</td>
        </tr>
        </table>

        <div style="width:60px; float:left"></div>
        <div style="float:left; clear:right;">
        <p>We are located at:<br />
        4502 Chapel Road<br />
        Fort Worth, Texas 76134</p>
        <p>Our phone number is: (817) 555-0143</p></div>
        <p><a href="doctrine.html">We Believe</a></p>
        <p><a href="directions.html">Directions</a></p>
        </div>

    <%ELSE

    END IF

        Response.Write(Line&vbCRLF)

LOOP
TStream.Close
%>
```

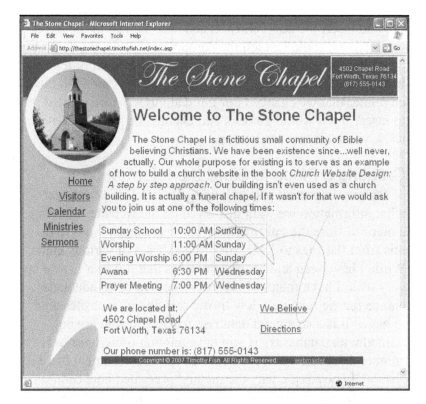

Once the new *index.asp* file is uploaded to the server and any mistakes have been corrected the *design.html* file can have the *home* anchor updated to link to the new index file. When you make the change to the *design.html* file and upload it to the server you will find that the correction is made in the *index.asp* file as well.

A New Way To Do Web Pages

Computers are wonderful machines when it comes to doing some of the things that we humans really don't enjoy doing. A computer can mindlessly repeat the same task over and over and over without mistake and without complaining. Humans dislike repetitive tasks and it is hard for us to do things the same way without mistake. Being able to specify the website appearance in one place and having a general purpose template in the *page.asp* file is better than what we had before, but it would be better if instead of having to copy the file and insert the new XHTML code for the rest of the pages we need, we could just tell the computer what we wanted it to insert the content and it would go off and do the work for us. It would be better if after we saw the result we could tell the computer that we changed our mind about what we wanted it to insert and it would go back and change the page. Let me show you have this can be done.

Creating a Place to Store the Information

A very important part of being able to tell the computer what information we want displayed on the website is having a place to store the information. There are many ways to do this from flat files to XML files to databases of various kinds. While I have seen and heard comments that it doesn't scale up very well, I have found Microsoft Access to be an adequate choice for the relatively low traffic that church websites tend to have. It is also a good database for people who are not trained with databases. If you have another preference or if another database will work better in your environment there is absolutely no reason why the method presented here cannot be modified to fit your environment, but it is beyond the scope of this book to explain how you may do so.

You can either create a new database using Microsoft Access or you can use the *thestonechapel.mdb* file and rename it to an appropriate name for your use. The database we need has only one table in it called **ARTICLE**. This table has twelve fields in it including *Id, Type, Title, Author, Date, Expire, Body, Approved, Hits, Keywords, Description,* and *AllowComments*. The *id* is the key and it will be used to specify the article through the URL. *Type* is arbitrary, but it can be used to distinguish between an article concerning a Sunday school class and one that is for the Senior Adult Ministry. *Title, Body, Keywords* and *Description* are the main ones we will be concerned with. The table design is in the screen shot shown here. Store the Microsoft Access files in the *cgi-bin* directory.

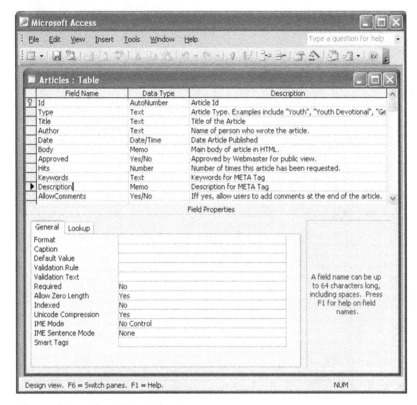

Reading the Database

If you copied *thestonechaple.mdb* your database will already be populated with some data. The heart of what we want to do with this database is to display this information our the website. To do this it is necessary to read the information from the database and use portions of it to replace sections of the code that is in the *page.asp* file.

The new file will be *article.asp*. It is shown on the next page.

```asp
<%'Reads a template, outputs everything but replaces the title, description and main text.
  'Copyright (c) 2007 Timothy Fish. All Rights Reserved.

set conn = server.createobject("ADODB.Connection")
conn.open "DRIVER={Microsoft Access Driver (*.mdb)};DBQ=C:\hshome\tdfish\thestonechapel.timothyfish.net\cgi-
bin\TheStoneChapel.mdb"

Dim rs, ListQuery, ArticleID
ArticleId = Request.QueryString("ID")
If ArticleId > 0 Then
ListQuery = "SELECT Article.Id, Article.Type, Article.Title, Article.Author, Article.Date, "&_
            "     Article.Expire, Article.Approved, Article.Body, Article.Hits"&_
            "     , Article.Keywords, Article.Description, Article.AllowComments" & _
            "     FROM Article" & _
            "     WHERE Article.Id = "&ArticleId&" And Article.Approved = TRUE;"

Set RS=conn.Execute(ListQuery)

strPathInfo = Request.ServerVariables("PATH_INFO")
Set FileSys=Server.CreateObject("Scripting.FileSystemObject")
Set TStream=FileSys.OpenTextFile("C:\hshome\tdfish\thestonechapel.timothyfish.net\design.html", 1)

DO WHILE TStream.AtEndOfStream <> True
    Line = TStream.ReadLine()
    IF InStr(1, Line,"<!---- Title and description go here! ---->",vbTextCompare) <> 0     THEN
%>
        <%If NOT RS.eof Then%>
        <title>
        <%IF RS("Expire")<>"" THEN
            IF RS("Expire") <Date THEN
                Response.Write("Archive:")
            END IF
```

```asp
        END IF%>
    <%=RS("Title")%></title>

<meta name="Keywords" content="<%=RS("Keywords")%>" />
<meta name="Description" content="<%=RS("Description")%>" />
        <%End If%>
<%ELSEIF InStr(1, Line, "<!----- Document text goes here! ----->") <> 0 THEN%>
        <%If NOT RS.eof Then%>
    <%Hits = RS("Hits")
            If Hits = "" Then
                Hits = 0
            End If

    HitsQuery = "UPDATE Article SET Article.Hits = "&Hits+1&_
                    " WHERE  ((Article.Id)="&RS("Id")&"));"

    conn.Execute(HitsQuery)
    %>

    <%IF RS("Expire")<>"" THEN
        IF RS("Expire")<Date THEN
        Response.Write("<p><i><b>NOTE:</b>This page has been archived. "&_
                "It may contain out of date information.</i></p><hr />")

        END IF
    END IF%>
        <%If RS.Fields("Title") <> "" Then%>
        <h1><%=RS.Fields("Title")%></h1>
        <%End If%>
        <%If RS.Fields("Author") <> "" Then%>
        <h3>Written By <%=RS.Fields("Author")%></h3>
        <%End If%>
        <%If RS.Fields("Date") <> "" Then%>
        <h4>Published <%=RS.Fields("Date")%></h4>
        <%End If%>

    <br />    <%=RS.Fields("Body")%>
```

```
<%Else%>
<h1>Selected Article Not Found</h1>
<p>The article was not found by the database query. This may be due to the article
id not being in the database or it the webmaster may not have approved the article
for publication.</p>
<%End If%>


<%      ELSE
                Response.Write(Line&vbCRLF)
        END IF

LOOP
TStream.Close
END IF
%>
<%
conn.Close
Set conn=Nothing
%>
```

You will need to change the underlined text to the corresponding files on your server for this too work in you environment. This code produces a page like the one shown here:

The code does three things of importance. It reads the article from the article from the table if it is there. If it isn't then it tells the user that it can't be found. It updates the hit counter for the article. This is important because we always want to know how many people are reading our articles and which ones they are reading. Finally, it outputs the data in the same locations as where we put our own data in the *index.html* file.

The Article List

If all we had was a viewer that could read articles from an Access database and display them in the format we have designed we would have a lot, but it would be very inconvenient to add and remove articles from the database. The Access database would have to be downloaded and uploaded from and to the server every time a change needed to be made. During this time there would be the chance that some of the users might be accessing the data and the hit counter would be incorrect after the database was uploaded. The hit counter wouldn't do a whole lot of good because the database would have to be downloaded before it could be read. Perhaps the worst thing would be that the database could get to be several megabytes in size and the repeated uploading and downloading would require time and bandwidth. It would be much better to be able to make the modifications we need through the website instead of on the local machine.

The first thing that we need is a list of articles. This list will tell us what is in the database and serve as the front end to the edit process. On your local machine, create a subfolder in your website folder called *Maintenance*. On the web server you will need to password protect this folder. You don't want any of the jerks who create viruses and send out spam to be able to access these files. If they do, your website will soon have filth on it that is not appropriate for a church website. Your hosting company will need to tell you the specific details of how to protect this folder.

In the *Maintenance* folder create a file called *index.asp*. Even though they are both based on *page.asp* this is a different file than the one that is in the parent directory, so you will need to be careful to distinguish between the two when you are working with them. The common name is required because they both are the default files of their respective directories.

Password Protecting a Web Folder

Read the documentation or ask your hosting company how to do this. For ServerGrid this is done through Web-Shell the file explorer program. It has a protect button at the bottom of the screen that goes to a screen that allows the folder to be selected and users with passwords defined. Before that they used a text file in the folder to define protection.

The *Maintenance/index.asp* file looks like the code presented here.

```asp
<%'Lists all articles for for edit, deletion or viewing.
'Reads a template, outputs everything but replaces the title, description and main text.
'Copyright (c) 2007 Timothy Fish. All Rights Reserved.

strPathInfo = Request.ServerVariables("PATH_INFO")
Set FileSys=Server.CreateObject("Scripting.FileSystemObject")
Set TStream=FileSys.OpenTextFile("C:\hshome\tdfish\thestonechapel.timothyfish.net\design.html", 1)

set conn = server.createobject("ADODB.Connection")
conn.open "DRIVER={Microsoft Access Driver (*.mdb)};DBQ=C:\hshome\tdfish\thestonechapel.timothyfish.net\cgi-bin\TheStoneChapel.mdb"
Dim rs, ListQuery

DO WHILE TStream.AtEndOfstream <> True
    Line = TStream.ReadLine()
    IF InStr(1, Line,"<!----- Title and description go here! ----->",vbTextCompare) <> 0  THEN%>
<title>The Stone Chapel - Articles</title>
<%ELSEIF InStr(1, Line, "<!----- Document text goes here! ----->") <> 0 THEN%>

<%If Request.QueryString("DEL") = "TRUE" AND Request.QueryString("ID") > 0 Then
    DelQuery = "DELETE Article.Id, Article.* "&_
               "FROM Article "&_
               "WHERE (((Article.Id)="&Request.QueryString("ID")&"));"
    conn.Execute(DelQuery)
End If%>
<h1>Articles</h1>
<a href="EditAdd.asp">Add Article</a><br />
<%ListQuery = "SELECT Article.Id, Article.Type, Article.Title, "&_
              Article.Author, Article.Date, Article.Expire, Article.Approved, Article.Hits" &  _
```

```asp
                " FROM Article;"
        Set RS=conn.Execute(ListQuery)
    %>
    <table id="Table1">
    <tr>
        <th></th>
        <th>Edit</th>
        <th>Delete</th>
        <th>Id</th>
        <th>Type</th>
        <th>Title</th>
        <th>Author</th>
        <th>Date</th>
        <th>Expires</th>
        <th>Hits</th>
    </tr>
    <%index = 0%>
    <% DO WHILE NOT RS.eof%>
    <%index = index + 1%>
    <tr>
    <td><%=index%>.</td>
    <td><a href="EditAdd.asp?ID=<%=RS.Fields("ID")%>">Edit</a></td>
    <td><a onclick="return confirmDelete('<%=Replace(RS("Title"), "'", "\'")%>', "'", "\'")%>') "
                href="Index.asp?DEL=TRUE&amp;ID=<%=RS.Fields("ID")%>">Del</a></td>
    <td><%=RS.Fields("Id")%></td>
    <td><%=RS.Fields("Type")%></td>
    <td>
    <a href="../Article.asp?ID=<%=RS.Fields("ID")%>"><%=RS.Fields("Title")%></a>
    </td>
    <td><%=RS.Fields("Author")%></td>
    <td><%=RS.Fields("Date")%></td>
    <td><%=RS.Fields("Expire")%></td>
    <td><%=RS("Hits")%></td>
```

```
</tr>
<%
    RS.MoveNext
    Loop
%>
</table>
<br />
<%    ELSE
        Response.Write(Line&vbCRLF)

        END IF

LOOP
TStream.Close
%>
<%
conn.Close
Set conn=Nothing
%>
```

Make the changes to the underline path in this code that you made in the *article.asp*. As a matter of flexability, if you have created another template other than the one indicated by *design.html* you can use it here and this page would have a different appearance than the others. The database, however, needs to be the same or the website will not work properly.

The code makes the table shown in the image below possible. The fourth article listed in the image is intended to be the article that is linked to by the Visitors navigation button on the left. To do this in Windows® one would need only to right click on the title, select "Copy Shortcut" and copy the link into the appropriate place in the *design.html* file as the *href* of the **<a></a>** tag.

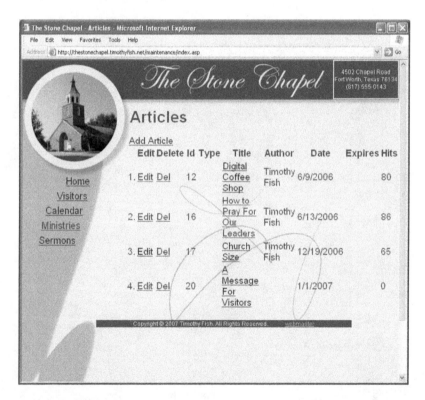

Adding Articles

At this point, articles can be deleted , but the *Add Article*, *Edit* links require an additional file in order to function. This file is called *EditAdd.asp*. Create this file in the maintenance folder. This file is a form that has most of the fields in the database. If no id is passed in then it will insert the data you submit. If an id is passed with the URL then it will edit. The form submits to itself, so the same page will show once the form is submitted. If the fields look like what you submitted then you know that the database is updated. If they revert to what they were or if they are different then you know that he database doesn't have the correct data.

The *Maintenance/EditAdd.asp* file should contain the code below. Be sure to make the appropriate file-name and path changes to the code.

```
<% 'Form to Edit or Add an article.
'Reads a template, outputs everything but replaces the title, description and main text.
'Copyright (c) 2007 Timothy Fish. All Rights Reserved.

strPathInfo = Request.ServerVariables("PATH_INFO")
Set FileSys=Server.CreateObject("Scripting.FileSystemObject")
Set TStream=FileSys.OpenTextFile("C:\hshome\tdfish\thestonechapel.timothyfish.net\design.html", 1)

set conn = server.createobject("ADODB.Connection")
conn.open "DRIVER={Microsoft Access Driver (*.mdb)};DBQ=C:\hshome\tdfish\thestonechapel.timothyfish.net\cgi-bin\TheStoneChapel.mdb"
Dim rs, ListQuery, ArticleID, ArticleType, Title, Author, PubDate, ExpDate, Body, Keywords, Description

DO WHILE TStream.AtEndOfStream <> True
    Line = TStream.ReadLine()
    IF InStr(1, Line,"<!----- Title and description go here! ----->",vbTextCompare) <> 0 THEN%>
    <title>The Stone Chapel - Edit Add</title>

<%ELSEIF InStr(1, Line, "<!----- Document text goes here! ----->") <> 0 THEN%>
<div style="float:left">
<%ArticleId = Request.QueryString("ID")
    Submittal = Request.QueryString("Submit")

    PubDate = Date

    If Submittal = "TRUE" Then
```

```
ArticleType = Request.Form("Type")
Title = Request.Form("Title")
Author = Request.Form("Author")
PubDate = Request.Form("PubDate")
ExpDate = Request.Form("ExpDate")
Body = Request.Form("Body")
Keywords = Request.Form("Keywords")
Description = Request.Form("Description")
IF PubDate = "" THEN
    PubDate = Date
END IF
IF ExpDate <> "" THEN
    EDate = "#"&ExpDate&"#"
ELSE
    EDate = "Null"
END IF
If ArticleId > 0 Then
    SubmitQuery = "UPDATE Article SET Article.Approved = True, "&_
              "  Article.Type = '"&Replace(ArticleType,"'","''")&"', Article.Title = '"&Replace
(Title, "'","''")&"', "&_
              "  Article.Author = '"&Replace(Author, "'","''")&"', Article.[Date] = #"&PubDate&"#,
"&_
              "  Article.Expire = "&EDate&", "&_
              "  Article.Body = '"&Replace(Body,"'","''")&"', "&_
              "  Article.Keywords = '"&Replace(Keywords,"'","''")&"', "&_
              "  Article.Description = '"&Replace(Description,"'","''")&"' "&_
              "  WHERE ((Article.Id)="&ArticleId&"));"

Else

    SubmitQuery = "INSERT INTO Article ( Approved, Type, Title, Author, [Date], Expire, Body, Keywords, De-
scription ) "&_
              "SELECT TRUE AS A, '"&Replace(ArticleType, "'", "''")&"' AS B, '"&_
```

```
                Replace(Title, "'", "''")&"' AS C, '"&Replace(Author, "'", "''") &_
&"' AS G, '"&_          "' AS D, #"&PubDate&"# AS E, "&EDate&" AS F, '"&Replace(Body, "'", "''")

&"' AS I;"             Replace(Keywords, "'", "''")&"' AS H, '"&Replace(Description, "'", "''")
            End If
            conn.Execute(SubmitQuery)

            If Not ArticleId > 0 Then
                SubmitQuery = "SELECT Max(Article.Id) AS A FROM Article;"
                Set RS = conn.Execute(SubmitQuery)
                If Not RS.eof Then
                    ArticleId = RS.Fields("A")
                Else
                    ArticleId = 0
                End If
            End If
            %>
            If ArticleId > 0 Then

            ListQuery = "SELECT Article.Id, Article.Type, Article.Title, Article.Author, Article.Date, Article.Expire, "&_
                    " Article.Approved, Article.Body, Article.Hits, Article.Keywords, Article.Description" & _
                    " FROM Article" & _
                    " WHERE Article.Id = "&ArticleId&";"

            'Response.Write(ListQuery)
            Set RS=conn.Execute(ListQuery)
            %>
                <%If NOT RS.eof Then%>
                    <%If RS.Fields("Title") <> "" Then
                        Title = RS.Fields("Title")
```

```asp
        End If%>
        <%If RS.Fields("Author") <> "" Then
        Author=RS.Fields("Author")
        End If%>
        <%If RS.Fields("Date") <> "" Then
        PubDate=RS.Fields("Date")
        End If%>
        <%If RS.Fields("Expire") <> "" Then
        ExpDate=RS.Fields("Expire")
        End If%>
        <%If RS.Fields("Type") <> "" Then
        ArticleType = RS.Fields("Type")
        End If%>
        <%Body=RS.Fields("Body")%>
        <%Hits=RS("Hits")%>
        <%If RS.Fields("Keywords") <> "" Then
        Keywords=RS.Fields("Keywords")
        End If%>
        <%
        Description=RS("Description")
        %>
        <%End If%>

<%End If%>
<h1>Add/Edit Article</h1>
<a href="index.asp">Goto List</a><br />
<p>Type article in form below. HTML formating is expected.</p>
<form
    id="Form1"
    method="post"
<%If ArticleId > 0 Then%>
    action="EditAdd.asp?Submit=TRUE&amp;ID=<%=ArticleId%>"
<%Else%>
    action="EditAdd.asp?Submit=TRUE"
```

```
<%End If%>
>
<p>Title: <input id="title" type="text" size="37"
value="<%=Replace(Title, """", "&quot;")%>" name="Title" /></p>
<p>Author: <input id="Author" type="text" size="34"
value="<%=Replace(Author, """", "&quot;")%>" name="Author" /></p>
<p>Date: <input id="PubDate" type="text" size="36"
value="<%=PubDate%>" name="PubDate" /></p>
<p>Expire: <input id="ExpDate" type="text" size="34"
value="<%=ExpDate%>" name="ExpDate" /></p>
<p>Type: <input id="Type" type="text" size="36" name="Type"
value="<%=Replace(ArticleType, """", "&quot;")%>" /></p>
<p>Body</p>
<p><textarea id="Body" name="Body" rows="12" cols="54"><%=Body%></textarea></p>
<p>           
<input id="Submit" type="submit" value="Submit" name="Submit" /
>          &n
bsp;          
;
<input id="Reset" type="reset" value="Reset" name="Reset" /></p>
<hr />
<p>Keywords: <input id="Keywords" type="text" size="36" name="Keywords"
value="<%=Replace(Keywords, """", "")%>" /></p>
<p>Description</p>
<p><textarea id="Description" name="Description" rows="12" cols="54"><%=Description%></textarea></p>
</form>
</div>
<%      ELSE
        Response.Write(Line&vbCRLF)
        END IF
LOOP
TStream.Close
%>
```

```
<%
conn.Close
Set conn=Nothing
%>
```

This code produces the form that is shown here. You may notice that the form doesn't follow the curve of the design.

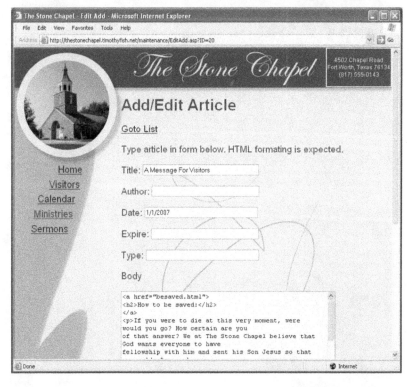

This is by choice. The form did not look attractive following the curve and even hid some of the navigation bar. Using a left floated division solved the problem and produced the result that you see.

The *body* field accepts XHTML code striped of the overhead. For example, the code `<p>Hello World!</p>` would produce a valid XHTML document because the ASP file will add the overhead.

The Finishing Touches

With all of these files coded and placed on the server, you are almost done with your first spiral of development. As time passes you will want to add new features to the site, but with just this much you can provide your users with any information that you might want to give them. There are just a few more things to do.

For the navigation links to work properly, we need to create an article for them and then update the *design.html* file. In the example, only *Ministries* does not have a valid link. To create one I will go to *http://thestonechapel.timothyfish.net/ Maintenance/* and type in my username and password. After that I click *Add Article*. This takes me to the form. I fill this with the information in the table. Do the same with your own website.

Title:	The Stone Chapel Ministries
Author:	
Date:	12/1/2007
Expire:	
Type:	
Body:	<div style="float:left"> <p>Awana</p><p>Sunday School</p><p>Visitation</p><p>WMA</p><p>Brotherhood</p> </div>
Keywords:	Stone Chapel, Ministries
Description:	See a list of the ministries at the fictional The Stone Chapel church.

The choice of a title and description is important. Many search engines use these values when displaying search results. You don't want people to see something like "Title Goes Here" or some random code from your site instead of a well written title and description. The keywords aren't used much for searching, but some tools put them to use so it is best to have them in place, just in case. A publication date is required and the rest is optional.

After I submit, I can go to the list and find that the new article is in the database. The link can be grabbed by doing a right click, "copy shortcut." This gives me *http://thestonechapel.timothyfish.net/Article.asp?ID=24*. This can be pasted into *design.html* to propagate this value to all pages.

```
<div class="Layout" id="Nav4">
<p>
<a
href="http://thestonechapel.timothyfish.net/Article.asp?ID=24"
>Ministries</a></p>
</div>
```

Once *design.html* is uploaded to the server the coding of the website is basically done. There are still plenty of articles that can be written, but everything except the links from the main *index.asp* can be done through the web form.

For the example, articles will need to be written for the links on the home page. There are two. One for doctrine and one for directions to the church.

Images will need to be uploaded. This should be JPEG or GIF files. You can use FTP to upload them like regular files. It is best to store them in a *images* directory since there may be several. Once they are there, you can specify either a URL or a relative path to them.

Step 9:
Testing the Website

*Bring ye all the tithes into the storehouse, that
there may be meat in mine house, and prove
me now herewith, saith the LORD of hosts, if I
will not open you the windows of heaven, and
pour you out a blessing, that there shall not be
room enough to receive it.*

$\qquad$ – *Malachi 3:10*

When all of the scripts are in place and all of the articles
have been written you may have a desire to declare yourself
done. You may want to sit back and bask in the glow of your
accomplishment as thousands of people use your site. Don't
sit there too long, one of the things that may be easy to over-
look in an all volunteer development environment is that complete testing needs to be done.

Testing isn't about showing how much better one person's
work is compared to another person's. Even if you developed
it yourself, it still needs to be tested. We all make mistakes
and when these mistakes are hidden in text documents that
have portions that won't be read for long periods of time or
may not be read at all, these mistakes may not be as obvious
as some of the other mistakes we make. The purpose of testing is to find mistakes so that they can be corrected before a
user inadvertently finds them.

The Things to be Tested

There are several things that should be tested before a website is considered releasable. Before any code was written there had to be some decisions about what the website was supposed to do. A more formal term for this is *requirements*. Tests should be done to verify that all of the requirements are met.

The requirements were fed into the design, but just because the website meets all of the requirements doesn't meant that it matches the design. The design may have included a better way of doing something, but it was left out during coding. Tests should be done to determine if everything in the design was pulled over into the website.

The code must also be tested. The links must be checked; the titles of the pages must be correct; the page text and images must be correct; if there are forms then they must function for all possible inputs; keyboard inputs must be checked.

Usability tests should be done with the final website. These tests help to determine if the site is easy to use for people who have never seen it as well as for the more experienced user. Do the testers have a good idea of what to click to get where they want to go? Do they get confused? Is the page hard for them to view? Does it look as good on their machine as yours?

Who Should Do the Testing

Someone else should do the testing. Every website developer tests his own code. Some testing has to be done by the developer or by someone who understands the code well enough to put it through its paces, but it is better if someone else does the testing.

One of the problems humans have is that we don't like to find that we have made a mistake. When testing our own creations we want to stay away from those things that have a high probability of causing them to fail because we like the feeling that they are perfect or we want to avoid the work of fixing them.

After spending hours working with the website, we may have learned paths through the errors that will never cause a problem. We might know that we intended for a field to have a value in it, so we always put a value there. The user doesn't know that and might put an incorrect value in the field or leave it blank. Because of our habits, we may fail to test this properly.

Look for volunteers in your church who are willing to test the website before it is released and/or announced. These people don't have to have a strong technical background. They should be told and reminded, when needed, that any mistakes that they find or make while using the website are not their fault. If a page loads with an error message or a person doesn't know what to enter, there may be the sense that it is his fault. Don't let your testers think this. Errors and usability problems need to be corrected by modifying the code and design rather than educating the user to follow the "correct" path.

How To Do The Testing

Some websites are easy to test. Some involve nothing more than clicking a few links, but even with the most simple websites there are many things to check.

Looking For Errors

One of the first things a tester should do is to get an overall feel for the site. The tester should spend a few minutes playing the part of an average user who might visit the site and try to answer some questions. What would the average user believe the main focus of the site to be? Which people might bookmark the page in order to find it later? Is it easy to find the information that users are likely to want? How much information is there that has little to do with the main point?

Once the basic flow of the site is checked, the tester should begin to do a systematic test of all of the pages in the site. The tester should read the text looking for mistakes such as spelling mistakes, grammatical errors and word usage problems. Every link on the page should be checked to see if it goes where it is supposed to go. The tester should follow the link and then hit the back button to go back to the previous page to continue testing. There may be an infinite number of paths through a website while there are only a finite number of pages. Staying with one page until it is completely tested will help to insure that all of the page is tested.

Some sites, such as the example site for this book, have navigation links that are supposed to be the same on every page. A tester will need to test these on every page. One page may look identical to another but it may be created by a different file or it may be in a different directory. When links use relative paths there is a risk that the developer will forget to change the path when a page is copied from one directory to another.

With ASP and other scripting languages it is possible to execute different code based on what a user enters into a form, the current date, the browser that the user has, the screen size or even a random number. These things make it harder to test everything. For a form, the tester should look at both normal input and mistakes that a user might make. If a user might leave a field blank then the tester should see what happens when some of the fields are blank. If the input has a range of values the tester should pick at list one value in the middle, one on the low end, one outside the range on the low end, one on the high end and one outside the range on the high end.

If a webpage is meant to behave differently for different browsers then more than one browser will need to be used to thoroughly test it. It is a good approach to always test code on different browsers. W3C defines the standards, but it is up to software companies and independent programmers to implement the browsers that behave by the standard. If a software company decides to ignore all or part of the standard then some users may see your website differently than what you intended. Unfortunately, it is your website that is seen as having made a mistake rather than the company that developed the browser. For this reason the website should be tested on, at least, the most popular browsers to verify that everything is readable even if things are a little off.

Testing code that is impacted by the current date can cause a problem. The date may not occur for several months. One solution is to change the code to a date that is current, test the website with that date and then change the date back to what it is supposed to be.

Random numbers can be handled in a similar fashion. The code could be changed to systematically test various numbers and then changed back to use the random number. This will not work in some cases because it is the randomness of the value that is important and the code will not function the same way with systematic testing.

Usability Testing

Usability testing is mainly about the human-computer interface. Websites are primarily a human-computer interface. When doing usability testing, the tester is looking for potential problems and for ways to improve the ease with which the user can interact with the computer.

One method that can be done to do usability testing is to have the user answer a questionnaire related to the ease of use of the website. If the website has errors and bad links then the answers on the questionnaire will indicate a low usability, so the questionnaire should be done after the other problems have been resolved.

The questionnaire should look for issues with load times, how hard it is to read the information, how hard it is to get the information that the user needs. It should ask about how intuitive the tester found the website to be.

Another method that can be used in usability testing is for someone to sit behind the tester and watch what he does as he moves through the site. Notes should be taken about how quickly he was able to find what he needed, what things he didn't understand and anything else that might indicate that he had trouble navigating and using the site.

Validating the XHTML

One of the things that was covered briefly in a previous step was the need to validate the XHTML that you create. Browsers are designed to be very forgiving, so if you make a mistake and put a tag in that is in uppercase instead of lower case or leave the paragraph tags off or forget to have the HTML tag at the beginning and end of the document, the browser will probably display it like you intended anyway. Since this is the case, you might be wondering why there is a need to validate the page.

Not all browsers handle nonstandard code in the same way. It is hard enough to get the software companies to handle standard tags in the way the standards organization intended. It is next to impossible for them to agree on what to do when the text files do not match the standard. Validating to the standard helps to insure that the end users will see what you intended for them to see.

W3C offers a XHTML validation tool at *validator.w3.org*. When using this tool it is possible to validate using the URI, the file location or by typing or pasting the XHTML text into the form. It is most helpful to use this tool during the coding process. This testing can be done after the site is developed, but it is harder to make changes when everything is already in place.

If you are using a tool to generate XHTML code it may not generate valid code, so the validator will fail. In order to insure that the validation will occur, you may have to go through the code and manually change how some of it is written. This isn't a lot of fun, so if you find that a tool you have isn't producing valid code you may decide to discontinue using the tool.

Step 10:
Deploy the Site

The next day John seeth Jesus coming unto him, and saith, Behold the Lamb of God, which taketh away the sin of the world.

– John 1:29

If you are following suggested approach and using the server as part of the development environment, the site has been available on the internet for some amount of time. Even so, if no one knew about it, it probably hasn't been seen by many people. It takes more than just making the site available online to deploy the website.

The Big Announcement

When the site is ready, you will want the rest of the church to know. The site is sitting there ready to go to work, but it will do little good for the church members if they don't know to find it. Even if they know where it is they won't bother unless they feel like there is a reason to look for it. You will have to tell them where to find the site and why it is important to them.

How you announce the release of the site will depend on the church. For small churches, a person might tell each person about the website and how to find it. It isn't necessary to tell everyone because the webmaster would know enough to know whether the person has access to the internet or not.

In a medium sized church the announcement might be done in the church bulletin. A small note or even a half page might be used to tell people where to find the site and the kind of information that is available on the site.

Another method that a medium sized church might use it to have someone mention it from the pulpit. This person could tell the people why this information is important to them. If this method is used it would still be good to provide people with the URL in printed form so that they can take it home with them. People generally have trouble remembering a URL unless they have used it often. Bookmarks work well because people tend to stuff them in their Bibles and they have to look at it again even if it is to throw it away.

The methods used in a medium sized church would also work in larger churches, but a larger church might have the funds available to buy promotional items with the URL on them. People are more likely to keep promotional items than they are to keep a printed sheet of paper. Imagine having people drinking out of a coffee mug with the church's URL printed on one side.

Remind people of the reasons why the church wants a website. If those reasons are good reasons then they will help encourage people to take a look at the site and to continue using it.

Also, show people how the website can help them personally. People are busy. It is not enough to show people that they need the website. There are many things that people need, but other things take priority.

Tell The World

If you want the world to visit your website you will have to tell them about it as well. Just like with encouraging people to attend church, they won't come if you don't invite them.

The Printed Media

There are several ways to tell people about your website. One thing you can do it put it on all of your printed material.

Put it on the church bulletin. If you have mail out bulletin, put it there. Put it on the church stationary. Anything that your church prints should have the website address on it. People should always know where they can get more information about the things your church is doing.

Because you will be encouraging people to gain more information from the website, you will need to make sure that your website stays up to date about anything that might be mentioned in you mailings. If people receive something in the mail and then go to the website only to find that the mailing is more accurate they will lose confidence in the website. The website it the easiest thing to change, so strive to make it the most accurate.

Use signs and banners. Driving along the freeways and highways you may have seen signs listing the website of a business or church. Some are on church signs. Some are on banners that hang from buildings. You may have even visited a few of the websites just to see what was there. Signs and banners work, even if they are just to point a person to a website. If you have this avenue available to you then you should definitely consider using it.

Back Links

A back-link is a link that another site has made to your site. Every time another webmaster links to your website you receive a double benefit in terms of increasing the traffic to your site. If a web surfer happens to be at the other site and clicks on the link, he will be taken to your site so in that way it is a direct benefit. Also you receive an indirect benefit in how your site appears on search engines.

Not every IP address is connected to a web site. In fact, the vast majority of IP addresses are not. It would not make sense for search engines to test each of the billions of IP addresses to see if it has anything in which web surfers might have an interest. Even if this approach was used, the search engine might not know how to access the information. The approach to indexing the web that is generally used is to follow links. This is called *crawling* because a *spider* crawls from page to page looking for information and links.

A search engine begins with a set of known web pages. The *spider* reads the latest version of the page from the web server and checks for new information, updating the database as it goes. If there are any links on the page then these links are added to the list of links the *spider* is scheduled to visit. Any duplicates are removed from the schedule. When the *spider* is done with a page it moves to the next link on the schedule. In time the *spider* will visit every page on the internet that has a link leading to it from an indexed page. Links from pages that are not indexed will do nothing to get the new page indexed. In the diagram shown here, the unknown page will

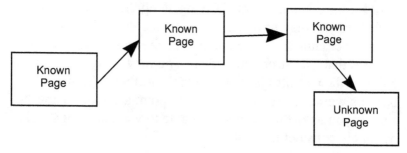

eventually be seen by the *spider* because it has back-links from known pages. In the case where an unknown page with back-links from other unknown pages there is no hope of it being seen by a search engine's *spider*, so it will not be indexed.

Back-links are very important in getting listed in search engines and increasing the rank-

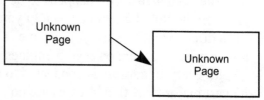

ing of your site's pages in the search engine results. Not only are back-links required for a page to be listed, but the number of back-links can serve as a kind of vote for a page from other pages on the internet. The more votes your page has, the more valuable it is considered by the search engines that use this as a gauge of importance.

Some hosting companies offer a service that promises to get your site listed in many search engines. Some promise listing in hundreds or thousands of search engines. This is mostly an unneeded service. If your site has as few as one back-link, the major search engines will find your site eventually. If it meets their requirements they will want to find your site and will list it for free. There is no need to pay for them to do so. The service that you may be buying through some of these sites may be to get back-links from a site that is linked to thousands of web pages. Having your site listed on pages that have a lot of links will not help your site much.

It may take months before you begin to see your website gain much notice in the search engine results. Patience is the key when it comes to dealing with a new website and search engines. Search engines want relevant data and new sites have a tendency to not be very relevant. A site that has stuck around and make frequent changes is more likely to have information the users of the search engines want to see.

There are some things that can be done to gain significance in the opinion of the search engines. Building a good set of back-links from sites that contain similar data to you own will significantly improve your search engine ranking in time. The *spider* software may use the link text, the text around the link, as well as the main text of the page to determine how relevant a page is to the user's query. Having link text that matches a user's query, text on the page that matches the user's query and text around the link that matches the user's query can help make your page more relevant in the eyes of the search engine. On the other hand, if the only thing that matches the user's query is the text in the document, but there are no links from relevant documents and the link text doesn't seem to fit, it would be logical for the search engine to provide another page that has more going for it than your page.

One place you can add back-links is on denominational or association websites. Many of these organizations link to the churches that are a part of their organization. This type of back-link can be considered a high quality back-link. On the other hand, there are other sites that allow links to be added for free. Some of these are nothing more than a long list of churches. Some sites will link to your site if you link to their site. Some sites will link to your site if you pay to be included. These back-links can be helpful if you have enough, but they are not as valuable as links from sites similar to your own.

Optimize the Site

Search engine optimization is an attempt to design your site in such a way that it looks more relevant to the search engines and so that when a user sees it in the search results he is more likely to click on it. There are several things that can be done that will help in this way. Some of these are designed into the methodology that is presented in this book.

Title Tag

Always put relevant text in the title tag. The title tag does more than just change the title at the top of the browser window. Search engines often use the title to tell their users what the page is. The search engines also use the title in their algorithms If the search words are in the title there is a greater change that it will be included in the results.

Use text that accurately describes the content of the document. Use words that a user is likely to type while looking for the page.

The articles database and ASP pages that were covered earlier were designed to have a unique title for each article. If good titles are used, the pages that are created will do better in the search results.

The URL

The choice of a domain name can influence how a page ranks in the search results. As you might expect, a page that has the search words in the URL is likely to get a boost in the ranking. If you can, get an URL with your church name in it. If you can't get that then get one that is descriptive of your church. Focus on words that people use in searches.

Directories and filenames are also part of the URL and can have an impact on the search results. If you are looking for information about apples you would expect that the information in a file with the path *apples/granny_smith.html* would be more relevant than one with the path *drinks/coffee.html*. Search engines are somewhat dumb, but they are designed to find words such as these and these words indicate relevance.

Special Tags

Make good use of hyperlinks as well as bold and italic text. The text that appears in special tags like headings, emphasis and strong emphasis can be a consideration in the search result rankings. Some search engines give higher importance to these words because they are considered important enough to add special tags.

Search Words

How often a term occurs in a document can be a consideration. The more it occurs, the more relevant the document seems for that subject.

Use words frequently that you want surfers to use when finding your site, but don't over do it. Work these words into the main body of the document. If words occur too frequently then the page looks like it lacks substance. If words occur too seldom then the page won't be considered.

Other words that are close to the search words can give a search engine information about what the site is about. If the search words are all close together then the page will appear more relevant to the search. If search words are right next to each other it is even better.

Words that are in the same order as what the user typed into the search engine the page may be considered to be more relevant.

Hidden Text

There are some kinds of text that are hidden to most users, but search engines make good use of it. Images have the *alt* attribute. This can be used in browsers that don't see images or for users who are blind. The *alt* attribute should contain text describing the image in short terms. These attributes can add text to the document without changing the layout. It also helps to add relevance because search engines are unable to read graphical text and need help to determine what the page is saying with graphics.

Spider software doesn't display anything so it has no need for frames. If your website uses frames (not recommended) you might find that the only pages listed has a title of "This browser does not support frames" or something similar. There is a way around this. The way around this is to create a copy of the page to go in the NOFRAMES tag. After doing this the *spider* will see the text you want it to see rather than the standard alternate text.

Develop Content

Search engine optimization involves the development of content that helps show the page to be relevant. This may include adding words to a document to increase frequency. It may include adding a page that frequently uses words related to the target audience.

The Unknown

Search engine optimization is more of an art than a science. If a person knew the exact algorithms that were used he might be able to manipulate the search engines more than they already are. But the search engine companies keep their algorithms and filters under tight wraps, so how much to do and what to do is mostly unknown.

Step 11:
Stay the Course

*Know ye not that they which run in a race run
all, but one receiveth the prize? So run, that ye
may obtain.*

– I Corinthians 9:24

We're done right? Unfortunately, I must say no. The
website is in place. It looks great. It is starting to show up in
the search engine results. People at church seem to be happy
with it. Someone outside the church has even contacted the
church after seeing the website. We have accomplished
something great so it is easy to think that it is time to move
on. This is not the case.

Maintenance: The Real Work

You may have spent days putting the website together.
Expect to spend many more days maintaining the site. The
time may be more spaced out, but many more days will be
required for maintenance.

Maintenance is anything that must be done to the website
to keep it up to date and in working order after it has been de-
ployed. In most software development projects, maintenance
burns more man-hours than all of the other phases combined.
A good church website, because of its nature, will require
much more.

If you used the website design that has been presented in this book then it is possible for your articles to go out of date without you needing to change anything. If you have a list of articles to show the user, you can filter out the archived articles and the user will only see the new stuff. It is not so simple for articles that have a direct link on one of the pages. The links will not just disappear when an article goes out of date. These will have to be updated. It will help if you make a practice of dating any new articles that link to dated material, but there will still be the occasional article that will have to be changed.

New articles will have to added. How often new articles need to be added is dependent on the purpose of your website. There are some things that never change or change very seldom. The doctrinal statement and the statement of how to be saved won't change much in a long time. The statement of how to be saved might change if you want to reword it, but it won't hurt if you leave it alone. Some things need to be changed on a annual basis. If a church elects officers and teachers on an annual basis then the website will have to be updated to reflect the officers and teachers that are elected. When a resignation or another change occurs, the website should be updated to reflect the change. There are other things that might require changes on a monthly or weekly schedule. If you are providing articles concerning current events, new articles are needed regularly. Sermon uploads should occur on a weekly basis unless you just want a few sermons or the best sermons uploaded.

When possible, code should be written to automate anything that must be done every week or every day. These are the things that will kill a church website very quickly. A business can pay someone to do something everyday, but volunteers are usually leery of something that requires a commitment to do something everyday. Volunteers have lives, families and other responsibilities. Some people are willing to put in a lot of effort for the church, but they will need time away from the tasks they do. People working in a web ministry need to feel free to work with it when they have time, leave it alone for several days and then go back without the whole thing snowballing into a bigger mess than what it was when they left.

A Work Schedule

One way to keep a handle on the work that needs to be done is to develop a work schedule. The following is a list of some of the things that are done with the *South Park Baptist Church* website.

- Upload Sermons (weekly)
- Update the church calendar (weekly)
- Check for relevant articles that can be reprinted (daily or every few days but can be skipped occasionally)
- Write an editorial (monthly)
- Write about things occurring at church (weekly or when things occur)
- Remove older sermons (every several weeks)
- Update information in existing articles and pages (when changes occur)

Some people like to do things when they think about them while others prefer to do thing things at the same time each week. As you can see, most of the things that are shown here could be scheduled for one day out of the week. A person might decide to dedicate Monday evening to working on the website. Anything that comes up during the week, unless it is pressing, could be written down on a to-do list and then when Monday rolled around it could be done at that time. You might also consider doing things when you get to them, but writing a to-do list for anything that you can't do right away will be helpful.

Most church websites have one person doing most of the work, but if you have several people then you might considered using an online list of things that need to be done. A person working on the website could pick one to do, do it and check it off the list when it is finished.

A weekly schedule might look like the following:

- Check church bulletin for changes to the church calendar and other announcements to add to the website.

- Check sources for relevant new material.
- Add new articles that are needed.
- Upload sermons, remove old ones if needed or desirable to do so.
- Respond to e-mail queries.
- Scan website for out of date links. Add to a list.
- Update at least some of the out of date links.

Make copies of your regular list of things to do. Each week you can go through and check off each item as you do it. Having a list will help you to remember to do some of the things that don't readily come to mind as something that needs to be done.

Version Control

You may not have realized it, but as you stepped through this book there was a limited amount of version control that was going on. Each step built on what had been done in previous steps. It would have been possible to have one directory that was modified as the website was developed, but instead you were asked to copy existing files and rename them. By doing this you were able to go back and look at a previous version.

It is a good practice to use some form or version control with your website. There are tools that you can use to automate this, but as a minimum you need to save all of the files that are on the server and put a version number with them. For a small website you may be able to store everything in one compressed file. Some sites might have to be stored to a CD or DVD. Sites that are larger than a few gigabytes will need to be handled differently, but few churches have sites this large.

If you are certain that a site hasn't changed then there is no need to make another copy of it, but websites are constantly changing. Adding a new article generates a different version of the website. It probably isn't necessary to archive every version that is created in this dynamic fashion, but periodically a copy should be made and stored as a new version.

Software changes should always be considered a new version and each version should be archived.

Keeping a copy of each version makes it possible to go back and look at what was working and what wasn't. Not every fix works the way we intended. It is good to be able to go back to a version that we know is working rather than having to rework the fixes until the code is working again.

Meeting Goals

Strive to reach your goals. Everyone who develops a website has some kind of goal in mind. It may be to increase church attendance. It may be to bring the church into the twenty-first century. It may be to provide a source of information. There are many goals that a person might have.

Realistic Goals

With so many possible goals, what goals are realistic for a church website? What factors need to be considered when determining if a goal is realistic?

The church is a local body. Every church is a local church. Every church ministry is a local ministry. Every missionary is a local missionary. Someone once defined missions as people sending people to reach people. Every church is to be about the business of reaching people. These people are specific individuals who live in a local community somewhere in the world. We reach these people by talking to them, standing by their side in their time of need. When people look for a church they don't look for a church on the other side of the world. Many times they won't even look for a church on the other side of town. People are looking for a church that can be there for them and help them. They are looking for a local church.

The web is a global entity. Nearly every URL begins with the letters *WWW*, World Wide Web. Part of the beauty of the web is that a person can be in nearly any part of the world and can still gain access to the very same pages to which he can gain access sitting at the computer in your home. A man in Korea can listen to the sermons of a pastor in Fort Worth,

Texas. I know, it has happened. A woman in Chicago and go to the same web site and ask a question. I know, it has happened. A person who is only a few block from the church can visit the same web site and know what is happening at church. I know, it has happened.

Web pages are a global entity that have a global readership while a church is a local organization serving the needs of local people. Web pages are among billions of pages competing for the attention of millions of people. A church is one of only a few in an area and is competing for the attention of only thousands or hundreds of people. For a church website to be effective, it needs to help the church reach the goals of the church. This means that the primary focus of the website must be local. In some ways, websites are better suited to reach a wide spread audience rather than reaching the people of a specific area. There may be a handful of people in every major city who are interested in one of the articles on the website, but it may not include any of the people within a few blocks of the church, so an article might be immensely popular but not do anything to help the church reach its goals.

One unrealistic goal is for the church website to be read by every person in the local community. The website may reach some of these people, but it will not reach all of them. It may not even reach most of them. Since you are reading this book, it is safe to assume that you have used the internet and may have used it quite a bit. Think about the things you have looked for on the internet. How many of these things were church related? How many of these things led you to a church that was in your local area? Now, since you, a person who is probably actively involved in church, are seldom directed to a local church website when you are searching the web, you can probably imagine how many times people who are not involved in church are going to find a local church website by chance.

If you provide tools that people can use, you can expect that your church members will visit your website, but don't expect all of them to visit, and only a few will make the site their home page.

If you fail to provide tools that people can use, the only time church members will visit the site is if they want to show someone where to find it. Even to get this to happen you will probably have to repeatedly encourage them to suggest that coworkers and other people check out the site.

One evening when I was out on visitation with another gentleman from our church I mentioned to a lady that she could listen to some of our pastors' sermons on our website. As we left, the gentleman told me that he did not realize that there were sermons on the website. It can be disheartening to realize that many church members who spend plenty of time looking at other things on the web haven't even taken the time to look at the church website, but it is a fact of life. Because of this many of the goals for what the website can do for church members may be unrealistic.

Website Statistics

Whatever goals we might have for the website, there must to be a way to determine if the goals are being met. One way of getting a picture of what is going on with the website is through the website statistics. Most hosting companies have some form of website statistics available to their customers. There is also software that is available to people who have their own servers.

Among other things, web statistics frequently show the following:

- Number of Visitors
- Number of Unique Visitors
- Number of Pages Requested
- Number of Hits
- Band Width
- Name of *Spiders*
- When the *Spider* Last Visited
- Which Pages Were Requested
- IP Addresses of Users
- Search Engine Used to Find the Site
- Query Used to Find the Site

When it is climbing, the *number of visitors* stat is the one that most webmasters like to see. When it is falling it is the one that makes one disappointed. This number is nothing more than the number of times a new session is started with the website.

The *number of unique visitors* is the number of unique IP addresses that visit the site. It is something of a guess because there is not a one-to-one correspondence between visitors and IP addresses. Still, it is close enough to tell us if we are getting a lot of return visitors or if most of them are first time visits for the month.

The *number of pages requested* gives an indication of whether people are clicking through to other pages or if they are getting the information they need from the first page they find. Each page amounts to being one click made by a user.

The *number of hits* and the *bandwidth* are primarily measures that can be used to improve performance. A *hit* is a request for a file. This file may be a page, but the individual images that are embedded into the page are also registered as hits. Include files are registered as hits. The *bandwidth* tells you how large of a request is being made. With all else constant, a lower *bandwidth* number will result in a faster response to user requests.

Search engines use *spiders* to index a site and the *spiders* have names. The name usually has the name of the search engine embedded in it so you can tell which search engines have indexed your site. The stats tell you when the *spider* last visited. Ideally, for the better search engines, you will see a date that matches the current date, but the last crawl may have occurred several days or weeks earlier. This is an indication that the *spider* doesn't think it needs to visit your site very frequently. This usually occurs if the pages don't change very often. *Spiders* are hungry for new data and you have to feed them if you want them to be your friend.

The stats can tell you which pages were requested. This probably won't be very helpful in the setup that was defined in this book. The website in this book is basically two pages.

Knowing that a user read an article is not a surprise since all of the pages are articles.

IP addresses can indicate a country of origin and can sometimes be traced back to a specific location. It is very rare that you will need this information for anything, but it is information that is readily available in the log files.

The information about which *search engine* a user used will help you to determine how well you are doing with optimizing the page for a specific search engine. It is also an indication of how much of the site is indexed by the search engine.

The *search query* can give you a lot of information. Many users will stumble across your site by typing a query into a search engine. One of the things these queries can tell you is whether you website is on target or not. If the queries match the kind of things that are in line with the goals you have set for the site then it is a good thing. If the queries are for other things then you should determine what needs to change.

I once saw a church website that photos of various events. In looking at their statistics I found that even though they had a high number of visitors they had a disproportionate number of people who had reached the site by typing into a search engine the phrase, "photos of pool parties." The website may have been reaching lost people through this but most likely the people who found the pictures they were looking for would look at the picture and then leave without ever seeing the message that the webmaster hoped to communicate.

Web statistics won't get rid of all of the guess work but they do provide information that can be used for analysis. Careful analysis must be done to determine what the web statistics might be indicating.

Encouraging Usage

If the goals aren't being met, it may be time to encourage more people to use the website. Sometimes this requires more creativity than what is required to design the website in the first place.

One way to encourage usage is to show up at church with camera in hand and tell everyone that the pictures will be on the website. People like looking at pictures. This approach will work a few times, but it won't create a sustained growth in usage.

If you think the main reason the site isn't being used is because people don't realize what the website has to offer then you might try something like a scavenger hunt. Offer a small reward for the first person who can correctly answer a set of questions that can only be answered using the website. The size of the reward is not that important. The reward is just to make it a competition. The chance to be the one person to collect a five dollar prize is enough to get people to do something quickly rather than putting it off and forgetting about it.

You can also look for *sticky* content. Content is considered sticky if people will come back to it again and again. The church calendar can be sticky, but having this information in other locations reduces the stickiness of the content. Games can be sticky but they are usually off target and do not help to attract the people that we really want. Community information can be sticky if it lists the events that are occurring in the community and is the best source of this information.

Staying Enthused

It is not always easy to stay enthused about working with the web ministry. There may be times that low traffic and church members that don't understand the need for the website will cause you to question if you should continue. Even worse you might just quit doing any work on the website and several months later realize that you have let it get out of hand.

If you reach a point were you are having trouble staying enthused about doing the work then it is time to remind yourself why you are involved in the web ministry. Before you say, "I'm doing it because I love Jesus" let me say that no one is questioning whether you love Jesus or not. The real question is why you are showing your love for Jesus through the web ministry and not using that time to support some other ministry.

The web ministry has an opportunity to take the church into more homes than any other outreach ministry. Where other ministries have to ask to be let into people's homes, the web ministry is invited. This makes it a powerful tool. At our church, more people are touched by the web ministry than any other ministry. That doesn't make it better than the other ministries, but it certainly makes it worthwhile.

The web ministry has an opportunity to assist others in their own ministries. Other ministries can be enhanced when they use the website to provide information or to gain information from people.

The things that the web ministry can accomplish are good things. Remind yourself of this fact if you reach a point that you might give up. Rather than focusing on all of the work that has to be done when you would prefer to be doing something else, focus on what you can accomplish and look for ways to accomplish these goals. This will help you to stay committed to the work and to stay the course until it is your time to move on to something else.

Prepare a Replacement

One of the things that many people in church ministries fail to do is to train a replacement to take their place when they leave, quite or die. Yet the Bible gives us plenty of examples of men who were used by God to designate a replacement. Moses had Joshua at his side during the forty years after the children of Israel left Egypt. Samuel anointed Saul. Elijah passed his mantel to Elisha. Jesus hand picked the twelve apostles and spend years training them. Paul saw Timothy as his son in the ministry and Timothy helped to strengthen the churches Paul started.

The web ministry is one ministry that will stay around for a long time. In many ways we are just seeing the beginning of what is possible. The technology may change but there will always be a need for people who understand the latest technology to use that technology to further the ministry given to the church. That is the heart of what the web ministry is about. The leaders of this ministry need to be aware that even though the ministry will be around a long time, it may not be God's will for them to remain in that ministry. Circumstances may dictate that you step down from the position of ministry leader, of webmaster or whatever position it is that you hold. When that time comes, it would be far better to have someone available to step in and continue the work than to let the ministry suffer. If there isn't someone then the ministry will suffer and all ground you gained may dwindle away.

Selecting a Replacement

Finding a replacement is not as easy as picking someone who thinks he knows a lot about computers. Finding a replacement requires some of the same consideration that went into you being chosen for the task. It is one thing to know about computers and another to be able to apply that knowledge in a useful way. The average video gamer knows a lot about computers, but that doesn't mean they know anything about maintaining a website or that they are willing to make a commitment and stick with it.

Praying is the best thing a person can do when looking for a replacement. Ask God to point you in the right direction. If you believe that the web ministry is an important ministry then you should have no trouble believing that God wants to lead you to the right person for that position. I trust that you do feel that the web ministry is important. If you don't you have no business being involved in it.

Developing a church website is not rocket science, so there is no absolute requirement that the person chosen to replace you have a computer science or graphical design background. Really there are more important things to consider. As you may have discovered in reading this book, anyone who is willing to learn can be taught to develop websites. It is more important that the person have a willingness, a passion, a calling to do the work than what it is that the person have the experience. There are plenty of people who might be willing to give it a shot just for the fun of learning something new or, in some cases, because they want to be recognized as a computer expert among their piers. Be careful when considering these people. I don't usually trust people who boast of knowing a lot about computers. If they really know something then they will talk about it like it is the most ordinary thing in the world instead of trying to show off what they know. I also don't trust people who agree to do something for me and never follow through on their promise. If the person can't do a simple task then he will have trouble taking on a bigger ministry. Likewise, a person who puts great importance on following through on the small things will put great importance on seeing that the ministry succeeds.

Training a Replacement

You should plan on a minimum of one month to train a replacement. Ideally, the person will have already been involved in the web ministry and just needs to step up to take over. Having someone already trained takes care of the unexpected scenarios in which you have to leave due to a sudden job transfer, you get mad and leave the church or you die. It is very difficult to train a replacement under any of these conditions.

Show your replacement what you do and explain why you do it. Make him very aware of how much work you put into the ministry on a weekly basis. Many people look at ministries and fail to see just how much work is required to make them successful. How many times has someone tried to teach a class and thought he could spend an hour on Sunday morning preparing for the class and be adequately prepared? If a successful teacher had shown him how to prepare a lesson then he wouldn't have made that mistake.

If you stay around, it may frustrate you that your replacement doesn't do things the same way as what you did. It is ok for him to do things differently. In fact, doing things different may help to improve the ministry. In training your replacement, don't try to tell him how to do things exactly the way you do. Instead, focus on showing him the most important goals of the ministry and why they need to be met. Then show him the methods that you used. Encourage him to try them and try some new things as well.

If there is time before you move on to other things, try to let your replacement take over the day-to-day tasks before you completely leave the web ministry. This will give him a chance to get his feet wet before he is totally baptized into the web ministry. Drowning someone in work first thing is not always a good idea. Offer to help later if you can, but once you leave the web ministry leave your replacement alone to do his own thing unless he specifically asks for your help.

A Half Step:
Some Parting Thoughts

He which testifieth these things saith, Surely I come quickly. Amen. Even so, come, Lord Jesus. The grace of our Lord Jesus Christ be with you all. Amen.

– Revelation 22:20, 21

There are many different ways that a website can be designed and there are many things that can be included or left out. What one person thinks is a good idea may be disliked by another. What one person views as attractive may be considered less so by someone else. Ultimately, it is up to you to decide what should and should not be included in your website. With that in mind, here are some of my thoughts concerning some of the things that you might consider.

Music and Other Audio Files

One of the things that some church webmasters include in their websites is music or short speeches that play automatically in the background or even the foreground. Most websites would be better off if they would leave out the background music. Most of the church websites that I have seen using this do it badly and it is very irritating. Instead of reading the content the users is scrambling to find a way to quiet the noise by either turning down the volume or clicking away from the website. We don't want users pressing the back button until after they have read the content. No matter how much you enjoy listening to "Amazing Grace" every time the website loads, other people are just looking for information and only want to listen to "Amazing Grace" when they have a desire to hear it.

If you do decide to use music that plays automatically, it should be quiet and non-intrusive. The music should be in a loop so that no matter how long the user stays at the site there isn't a break in the music. The music should set the tone of the visit and be consistent with the visual appearance of the site. If the site has a conservative design, go with conservative music. If the site has fun colors then go with something more upbeat. But, whatever you do, don't offend the user.

If you want to provide a talking head with (or without) a video, don't play the video automatically. Allow the user to choose whether to listen or watch the video. The user may not want to download that much data. A simple control that allows the user to click play to begin the video is sufficient and it will not irritate the user as much as the shock of the voice of a stranger suddenly coming through the computer speakers.

Guest Books and Text Input

While having user feedback can be a good thing, guest books and other free text input fields are an open invitation to evil and filthy minded people to sell anything from illegal medicines to sexually explicit images and videos.

A church website should never allow just anyone to add content of any kind. Checks should be in place to prevent bad content from appearing on the site. One way to do this is to store user supplied content and not display it until it has been approved for publication on the site. Some people use randomly generated codes that are hard for computers to read in order to insure that people entering content cannot use a computer to enter large amounts of data into the form.

Photos

Church websites look better if there are lots of smiling faces to show how excited people are to be attending church. Be careful not to assume that every photo can be used for any purpose. Some of the photos on a website are of an editorial nature, meaning that they tell about something. You might have an article about a youth mission trip and show images that were taken during the trip. A social event might have been held and you want to show images from that event. Because these photos are telling about the event or about the person in the photo, the use of them is protected under the first amendment. There are exceptions, but a camera shy person can't, on a whim, prevent you from using photos to tell what needs to be told.

There are other types of photos that might appear on a church website. These photos are decorative. While they may be intended to tell something, the thing they are telling is not directly related to the photo, so it is no longer considered an editorial use. Using photos in this way may require the permission of the people who are in the photo. Royalty free photos can be purchased from photographers who have obtained this permission from the subjects, but these photos can be expensive. If you are considering using pictures of church members, church guests or anyone else, it is best to ask permission. If someone says no then don't use the photo. Even if the use is of an editorial nature it is better to avoid using the image if it is possible to do so and clearly state what needs to be said.

Outsourcing

In this book, I have recommended outsourcing such things as calendars and sermon hosting because it reduces the amount of work required to produce a functioning website. There are some advantages to having control of these things, so if you have the time and the ability, I strongly recommend integrating these features into your site rather than providing links to other sites.

One of the things that I like about having control of the calendar database is that the whole website can serve as the calendar rather than just having one page that contains the upcoming events. I like to be able to display current events on every page of the site so that people know what and when things are happening, whether they check the calendar, visit the home page or come to the site by some other means.

All things come at a price. Using other sites might bring undesirable advertising, a monthly fee or a user agreement that is either restrictive or that gives away the intellectual rights to the data that is placed on the server. For some things this is alright but for others it can be a problem. If the church website is handling the details of the calendar, the articles, the sermons, the videos and anything else that might be placed on the site then there is not as much of an issue.

Keep Learning

This book is intended as a starting point. If you have typed in the code for each of the examples then you should have enough of an understanding to build your own website, but there are many things that can be done with websites that has not been covered in this book.

You should have enough knowledge to be able to look at websites and other books and with them gain more understanding. If you are considering learning more, I would recommend getting a book covering the topic of Active Server Pages. The W3C website (*http://www.w3.org*) is also worth some time.

Appendix A:
XHTML 1.1

The World Wide Web Consortium (W3C) is the standards organization that defines the standards that are used for web related technologies. Among the standards they have developed is a standard for XHTML and previously they developed the standard for HTML. HTML 4 removed many of the presentation tags that were added after a *de facto* standard developed and HTML began to move away from the concept of separating information from presentation. XHTML 1.0 was the first of the XHTML standards and was a reformulation of HTML 4 using XML. XHTML 1.1 is very much like the strictest version of XHTML 1.0 but there are some differences and it serves as a basis for modularized XHTML.

The information contained here is extracted from information that is provided by the W3C at *www.w3.org*.

Tags

XHTML documents contain many tags that are used to mark up the text information that composes their content. These tags are used to specify the purpose of each text item. Tags normally have an opening and closing tag such as the following:

****Some Text Here****

Some tags are used without textual content. XHTML 1.1 requires the use of a closing tag or a shorthand method to indicate that the closing tag is not needed. The following are both possible ways of doing this:

<span></span>
Or
<span/>

Tags are nearly always nested within other tags such as the following:

<span><a href="index.html">Link Text**</a></span>**

Text

Text that is between opening and closing tags in XHTML has some specific properties. Successive white space is treated the same as a single white space character. Adding spaces or a carriage return will result in one space being added between words no matter how many are inserted. Some characters are considered special because they are used to distinguish XHTML tags from regular text. Using the less than (<) or greater than (>) symbols can cause a browser to become confused and try to read the text as an XHTML tag. In normal text, the < and > character sequences should be used if it is intended that the user see these characters.

Some special characters have names like the ones above. They take on the form of &name; in the code. The table on the next page shows some of the more commonly used names.

It is easier to remember the names, but the characters in the table and the other characters in the ISO character set can be displayed using the sequence &#nnn, where nnn is the code of the ISO character.

Attributes

The attributes of a tag provide specific information. In the anchor tag it is necessary to know where the link goes so the *href* attribute is used like:

<a href="linkpage.html">Link to me**</a>**

Name	Symbol	Description
&quot;	"	Quotation Mark
&amp;	&	Ampersand
&lt;	<	Less Than
&gt;	>	Greater Than
		Non-breaking Space
&cent;	¢	Cent Sign
&pound;	£	Pound Sign
&copy;	©	Copyright
&reg;	®	Registered Trademark
&plusmn;	±	Plus or Minus
&sup1;	^{1}	Superscript 1
&sup2;	^{2}	Superscript 2
&sup3;	^{3}	Superscript 3
&para;	¶	Paragraph
&frac14;	¼	One-fourth
&frac12;	½	One-half
&frac34;	¾	Three-fourths
&iquest;	¿	Inverted question-mark

In this example, *href* is an attribute that states that the text should take the user to the specificed page.

Some attributes are used by nearly all of the XHTML tags. There are some exceptions but most tags use *class, id, title, xml:space, xml:lang, onclick, ondblclick, onmousedown, onmouseup, onmouseover, onmousemove, onmouseout, onkeypress, onkeydown, onkeyup* and *style*. *Class* specifies the class of the entity. *Id* specifies the unique identifier. *Title* is frequently used to provide a tool-tip type help. *Style* is the inline style sheet for the tag.

Document Structure

The XHTML 1.1 standard divided tags into groupings called modules. The Structure Module provides the tags that make up the structure from which the rest of the document hangs.

As a bare minimum an XHTML 1.1 document should look like the following:

```
<?xml version="1.0" encoding="UTF-8"?>
<!DOCTYPE html PUBLIC "-//W3C//DTD XHTML 1.1//EN"
    "http://www.w3.org/TR/xhtml11/DTD/xhtml11.dtd">
<html xmlns="http://www.w3.org/1999/xhtml" xml:lang="en" >
  <head>
    <title>Virtual Library</title>
  </head>
  <body>
  </body>
</html>
```

The following are not XHTML tags:

```
<?xml version="1.0" encoding="UTF-8"?>
<!DOCTYPE html PUBLIC "-//W3C//DTD XHTML 1.1//EN"
    "http://www.w3.org/TR/xhtml11/DTD/xhtml11.dtd">
```

These tags provide information about the XHTML document and the standard by which it should be judged.

<html></html>

This tag encloses the document. Every XHTML document must have these tags and all other tags must fall between them.

Attributes:

Non-standard, the following are allowed.
Xml:lang, id, profile, version,
xmlns="http://www.w3.org/1999/xhtml"

<head></head>

This tag provides information about the document as well as general style and formatting information. Other tags are needed to provide the details.

Attributes:

Non-standard, the following are allowed.

Xml:lang, id, profile

<title></title>

This tag is to be enclosed in the **<head></head>** tags. It provides the title of the page. The title is used by search engines when building search results.

Attributes:

Non-standard, the following are allowed.

Xml:lang, id

<body></body>

This tag holds the main body of information within the XHTML document. Only headings (**h1, h2, h3, h4, h5, h6**), blocks (**address, blockquote, div, p, pre**) and lists (**dl, ol, ul**) are allowed at the highest level of this section. All other tags must be enclosed within the permitted tags.

Attributes:

The standard common attributes are allowed.

Text

The text module contains the basic text container tags.

<abbr></abbr>

This tag indicates an abbreviation in the text.

Attributes:

The standard common attributes are allowed.

Example:

```
<abbr>Ln.</abbr> is the abbreviation of Lane.
```

<acronym></acronym>

This tag indicates that a word is an acronym.

Attributes:

The standard common attributes are allowed.

Example:

```
<acronym>MTBF</acronym> is an acronym for Mean Time Between
Failures.
```

<address></address>

This tag indicates an address in the text.

Attributes:

The standard common attributes are allowed.

Example:

```
    His address is <address>504 Carroll Street</address>.
```

<blockquote></blockquote>

This tag designates a paragraph as a block quote. Browsers will normally display a block quote as a block of text that is indented from the normal flow.

Attributes:

The standard common attributes are allowed.

The *cite* attribute is also allowed to specify a web page source of the quote.

Example:

```
<p>In his speech, the man said the following:</p>
<blockquote>Good evening ladies and gentlemen.  The time has
now come and it will not soon pass in which we must decide
what the Lord wants us to do and we must do it.  Too long have
we tried to do what we thought was right without considering
that the Lord has told us in his Holy Word.  We must go back
and learn those things that he has taught.</blockquote>
```

This code will display something like this:

In his speech, the man said the following:

Good evening ladies and gentlemen. The time has now come and it will not soon pass in which we must decide what the Lord wants us to do and we must do it. Too long have we tried to do what we thought was right without considering that the Lord has told us in his Holy Word. We must go back and learn those things that he has taught.

*
*

This tag puts a break in a line of text. It is used when a break is needed within a paragraph or another block that should be in a specific position. A break is always done with one tag because it contains no text.

Attributes:
Non-standard, the following attributes are allowed: *xml:space*, *class*, *id*, *title*

Example:
```
<p> Poetry is a form of writing<br/>
In which paragraphs<br/>
Are often broken.</p>
```

Will produce:

Poetry is a form of writing
In which paragraphs
Are often broken.

Rather than:

Poetry is a form of writing In which paragraphs are often broken.

<cite></cite>

This tag indicates that the enclosed text is a citation.

Attributes:
The standard common attributes are allowed.

\<code\>\</code\>

This tag indicates that the enclosed text is computer code.

Attributes:

The standard common attributes are allowed.

\<dfn\>\</dfn\>

This tag indicates that the enclosed text is a definition.

Attributes:

The standard common attributes are allowed.

\<div\>\</div\>

This tag indicates a division in the text. When combined with style sheets it is often used to create a block of text that is displayed in a specific location on the page.

Attributes:

The standard common attributes are allowed.

Example:

```
<div class="div1">This text is part of division one.</div>
```

\<em\>\</em\>

This tag indicates that the text is emphasized for importance.

Attributes:

The standard common attributes are allowed.

Heading Tags

The tags \<h1\>\</h1\>, \<h2\>\</h2\>, \<h3\>\</h3\>, \<h4\>\</h4\>, \<h5\>\</h5\> and \<h6\>\</h6\> are used to indicate level for a hierarchal document. They should be used for this purpose and not as a means to produce larger or smaller text.

Attributes:

The standard common attributes are allowed.

Example:

```
<h1>Chapter One</h1>
<h2>Topic 1:Some Topic</h2>
<p>This is the text of topic 1</p>
<h3>Subtopic 1.1</h3>
<h3>Subtopic 1.2</h3>
<h2>Topic 2:Another Topic</h2>
<p>More Text</p>
```

Will produce something like,

Chapter One

Topic 1:Some Topic

This is the text of topic 1

Subtopic 1.1

Subtopic 1.2

Topic 2:Another Topic

More Text

<kbd></kbd>

This tag indicates that the text is something that should be entered using the keyboard.

Attributes:

The standard common attributes are allowed.

Example:

```
<p>Type <kbd>RUN</kbd> in the box.</p>
```

Might produce,

Type RUN in the box.

<p></p>

This tag indicates that the enclosed text is to be treated as a paragraph. Paragraphs are normally separated by a break of some kind.

Attributes:
The standard common attributes are allowed.

<pre></pre>

This tag indicates that the enclosed text is preformatted, so spaces and line breaks should be preserved rather than replacing spaces and line breaks with a single space.

Attributes:
The standard common attributes are allowed.

Example:
```
          <pre>This text has 5      spaces and a line
break.</pre>
```

Produces,

This text has 5   spaces and a line
break.

<q></q>

This tag indicates a short quotation and should be rendered with delimiting quotation marks. Some browsers support this and others do not.

Attributes:
The standard common attributes are allowed. Additionally, the *cite* attribute is allowed for indicating a web source of the information.

<samp></samp>

This tag indicates that the enclosed text is a sample taken from computer code.

Attributes:

The standard common attributes are allowed.

<span></span>

This tag is an inline tag that allows styles to be used on specific letters, words, phrases or groups of sentences in a paragraph.

Attributes:

The standard common attributes are allowed.

Example:

```
<p>The <span class="animal">cow</span> is big.</p>
```

<strong></strong>

This tag indicates that the text should be rendered with strong emphasis. This usually done with bold or if spoken it might be said louder.

Attributes:

The standard common attributes are allowed.

<var></var>

This tag indicates that the text is a variable such as the ones that might be used in mathematics or computer code.

Attributes:

The standard common attributes are allowed.

Hypertext

The hypertext module is for creating hypertext links. It contains one tag.

<a></a>

The anchor tag is part of the hypertext module. When used, the anchor tag indicates that the enclosed text or image should be treated as a hyperlink. When the user clicks on this text the browser will load the referenced page.

Attributes:

The standard common attributes are allowed and the following are allowed:

accesskey

Indicates a single character that may be used to trigger the hyperlink using the keyboard.

charset

Indicates the character set of the target URL.

href

Specifies the target URL. This is required.

hreflang

Indicates the language of the target URL.

rel

Indicates the relevance of the target URL in relation to the current page. Standard relevance indicators include, *index, glossary, copyright, chapter, section, subsection, appendix, help, bookmark*. Things such as *next* or *prev* might also be used.

rev

Indicates the relevance of the current page in relation to the target URL. Standard relevance indicators include, *index, glossary, copyright, chapter, section, subsection, appendix, help, bookmark*. Things such as *next* or *prev* might also be used.

tabindex

Indicates the tab order position.

type

Indicates the content type.

coords

Provides the coordinates for an image map.

shape

Possible values are "rect", "circle", "poly", "default". This are provided for support of client-side image maps.

Example 1:

```
<p>Go to <a href="another.htm">another page</a>.</p>
```

Example 2:

The anchor tag can be used with named XHTML elements to link to a location within a document.

```
<p name="par1">This next link with take you to the next
paragraph. <a href="#par2">link</a></p>
<p name="par2">This will take you back. <a href="#par1">link
</a></p>
<p name="par3">This will take you to another paragraph on
another page. <a href="another.html#par4">link</a><p>
```

Lists

There are three types of lists that are supported by XHTML 1.1. These are *unordered*, *ordered* and *definition*. When used, these structure information in the form of a list and place the list in the flow of the document.

Attributes

The standard common attributes are allowed for list tags.

Unordered Lists

Unordered lists are formed using the <ul></ul> tags. Only the <li></li> tags (list item) are allowed at the highest level and the list text is included in the list item tags.

Example:
```
<ul>
<li>Apple</li>
<li>Orange</li>
<li>Graphfruit</li>
</ul>
```

Ordered Lists

Ordered list are used when some form of numbering is needed to show that the order is important. The <ol></ol> tags indicate the list and only the <li></li> tags are allowed at the highest level. The list text is included in the list item tags.

Example:
```
<ol>
<li>Go south five blocks</li>
<li>Turn left</li>
<li>Go two more blocks</li>
</ol>
```

Definitions

A definition is a list in which terms are listed with their respective definitions. The <dl></dl> tags begin and end the list. The <dt></dt> (term) and the <dd></dd> (definition) tags are allowed at the highest level. The list items might be definitions like are found in a glossary or they might be something other than definitions that should be displayed in a similar fashion.

Example:
```
<dl>
<dt>Groceries</dt>
<dd>Milk, Eggs, Bacon</dd>
<dt>Office Supplies</dt>
<dd>Paper, Ink</dd>
</dl>
```
Might result in,

Groceries
     Milk, Eggs, Bacon
Office Supplies
     Paper, Ink

Objects and Images

Web pages are more than just text. The object module and the image module allow other things to be included in the document. Objects are a wide range of things that could include such things as images and applets while images are limited in their scope.

<object></object>

The object tag declares an embedded object. The <param/> tag is used to declare runtime parameters. The object tag can be used in either the head or the body of the document. The text between the two tags is to specify the alternate text for browsers that cannot display the object.

Attributes:

The standard common attributes are allowed along with *declare, classid, codebase, data, type, codetype, archive, standby, height, width, name, tabindex.*

The *usemap* attribute is added to allow client-side image map capability.

<param/>

The parameter tag allows named values to be passed to the object. For example, an object might have a color or a another initial setting that could be specified.

Attributes:

The standard common attributes are allowed. There is a *name* attribute that is required. There are also *value, valuetype* and *type* attributes.

<img/>

The image declares an image to be displayed.

Attributes:

The standard common attributes are allowed. There are two required attributes. *src* specifies the URL of the image file. *alt* provides text to display if the image cannot be shown. The *alt* attribute should be a short description of the image. The attributes *height* and *width* specify the size of the area in which the image is to be displayed. Better results are obtained by ignoring these and using images that are correctly sized. The *longdesc* attribute specifies a URL of a page that describes the image in detail.

The *ismap* attribute defines the image as a server-side image map. The *usemap* attribute specifies which map to use when using client-side image maps. The *id* of the map is specified.

<map></map>

The map tag specifies an image map. The map is broken into areas that will take the user to different locations when clicked or not at all. The area tag is used between the map tags to specify different areas and URLs.

Attributes:
xml:lang, Event Attributes, *class*, *id*, *title*.

<area/>

The area tag specifies an area of an image to be a hyperlink to another URL.

Attributes:
The standard common attributes are supported with others.

href
Specifies a destination URL.

shape
Specifies the shape of the area. Valid values are "rect", "circle", "poly" and "default".

coords

Gives parameters for the shape. For a rectangle the order is left, top, right, bottom. For a circle the order is x center, y center, radius. For a polygon the order is x0, y0, x1, y1,...,xn, yn.

nohref

Specifies whether the area is to be included in the image map or not.

alt

This attribute is required. It specifies alternate text for the area.

tabindex

This attribute specifies tab order for the page.

accesskey

This attribute provides a means of keyboard input to follow the link.

Presentation, Edit and Bidirectional

These tags serve as modifiers that are primarily concerned with how the text is presented to the user.

<b></b>

This tag indicates that the text should be **bold**.

<bdo></bdo>

This tag indicates that the text should be presented from right to left (tfel ot thgir) rather than left to right. Hebrew text might be presented in this way.

<big></big>

This tag indicates that the text should be big, rather than the normal size.

<del></del>

This tag indicates that the text has been ~~deleted~~. This might be used in collaboration type exercises.

<hr/>

This tag adds a horizontal line from one edge to the other to the flow. It will begin at the left side of the division and extend to the right side.

<i></i>

This tag indicates that the text should be displayed in *italic*.

<ins></ins>

This tag indicates that the text has been <u>added</u> to the document.

<small></small>

This tag indicates that the text should be displayed small rather than normal size.

**

This tag indicates that the text should be a subscript$_{sub}$.

**

This tag indicates that the text should be a superscript^{super}.

<tt></tt>

This tag indicates that the text should be displayed as `teletype or fixed space text.`

Forms

A form is a way to request information from the user. To be truly useful, there needs to be some kind of computer program to read the form and handle the user's input. XHTML provides the capability to display the form to the user and to pass the form to a script. What is done after that is out of its scope.

Forms have a **<form></form>** tag and several other tags that are contained in this tag and define the input fields.

<button></button>

This tag creates a push button on the form. The text between the tags serves as the button text.

Attributes

The standard common attributes are handled with *name, value, type* (button, submit, reset), *disabled, tabindex, accesskey*.

<fieldset></fieldset>

This tag groups sets of inputs within a box with a border drawn around it.

Attributes

The standard common attributes are handled.

<form></form>

This tag is the parent tag for the form tags. It specifies where the information is to be sent. All of the other tags must be within these tags or the information will not be sent properly.

Attributes

The standard common attributes are handled with others.

action

This attribute is required. It specifies the URL that is to receive the data from the form.

method

This attribute can be either *get* or *post*. The default is *get*. When *get* is used, the data is sent as part of the URL of the target page. When *post* is used, the data is sent as the body of the request. The *post* method handles more data than the *get* method, but the *get* method can usually be bookmarked.

enctype
This attribute specifies the encoding type for the request.

accept-charset
This is a comma separated list of the possible character sets for the form.

accept
This is a comma separated list of content types that the server that is to process the form can handle.

<input/>

The input tag specifies a field in which the user can enter data.

Attributes
The standard common attributes are used as well as *type* (text, password, checkbox, radio, submit, reset, hidden), *name, value, checked, size, maxlength, src, tabindex, access-key*.

<label></label>

This tag attaches a text label to a form control. Clicking on the label should work the same as if the control was clicked. This is normally used with things like radio buttons.

Attributes
The standard common attributes are used along with *for* which specifies the *id* of the control. The *accesskey* attribute is also available.

<select></select>

When used with the option tag and the **optgroup** tag, this tag provides a selection list from which the user may choose items.

Attributes

The standard common attributes are used. Also used are *name, size, multiple* and *tabindex.*

<optgroup></optgroup>

This tag can be used to group options into related groups so that the user can find them in a lengthy list.

Attributes

The standard common attributes are used. The *disabled* attribute can be used to disable the grouping. The *name* attribute is required.

<option></option>

The text between these tags is the text that will appear in the containing selection list.

Attributes

The standard common attributes are accepted. Also accepted are *selected, disabled, label* and *value.*

<textarea></textarea>

This tag specifies an area where the user can input text. The text between the tags is the default text for the area.

Attributes

The standard common attributes are accepted. Also accepted are *name, rows, cols, disabled, readonly, tabindex* and *accesskey.*

Tables

Tables in XHTML are made up of rows of data. Columns exist in that each row has some number of individual elements. The table has the same number of columns as the number of elements in the longest row. All table elements must be placed within the table tags.

<caption></caption>

This tag specifies the enclosed text as a caption for the table. Style sheets can be used to specify the positioning of this caption.

Attributes

The standard common attributes are supported.

<col/>

This tag specifies attributes for a column in the table. It can be used in the table or colgroup.

Attributes

The standard common attributes are supported with *align* (left, center, right, justify, char), *char, charoff, valign* (top, middle, bottom, baseline), *span, width*. The *char* attribute specifies a character, such as a period or comma, that should be used for alignment. This attribute should only be used with *align="char"*. The *charoff* attribute sets the offset from the chosen character. *Span* is the number of columns. *Width* is the width the column should be.

<colgroup></colgroup>

This tag groups sets of columns for formatting.

Attributes

The standard common attributes are supported with *align* (left, center, right, justify, char), *char, charoff, valign* (top, middle, bottom, baseline), *span, width*. The *char* attribute specifies a character, such as a period or comma, that should be used for alignment. This attribute should only be used with *align="char"*. The *charoff* attribute sets the offset from the chosen character. *Span* is the number of columns. *Width* is the width the column should be.

<table></table>

This tag is the parent tag for the table.

Attributes

The standard common attributes apply. Also supported are *summary*, *width*, *border*, *frame* (void, above, below, hsides, lhs, rhs, vsides, box, border), *rules* (none, groups, rows, cols, all), *cellspacing* and *cellpadding*.

Header, Body, Footer

In XHTML a table can have a header, a body and a footer. These sections are subsections of the table that make it possible to treat each section somewhat differently. The tags that make this possible are **<thead></thead>**, **<tbody></tbody>** and **<tfoot></tfoot>**.

Attributes

The standard common attributes apply. Other attributes are *align* (left, center, right, justify, char), *char*, *charoff* and *valign* (top, middle, bottom, baseline).

<tr></tr>

This tag is used to mark a row of data. Each row is marked this way.

Attributes

The standard common attributes apply. Other attributes are *align* (left, center, right, justify, char), *char*, *charoff* and *valign* (top, middle, bottom, baseline).

<th></th> and <td></td>

The table header and table data are identical except in the way they are treated by the browser. Each marks a element in the table, but the table header information is displayed differently in a way that shows it to be describing the data rather than being part of the data.

Attributes

The standard common attributes apply. Other attributes are *abbr*, *axis*, *headers*, *scope* (row, col, rowgroup, colgroup), *rowspan* (covers more than one row), *colspan* (covers more than one column), *align* (left, center, right, justify, char), *char*, *charoff* and *valign* (top, middle, bottom, baseline).

Head Tags

The tags listed here come from different modules but they are placed in the head of an XHTML document.

<meta/>

This tag provides meta-information about the document.

Attributes

The meta tag supports *xml:lang*, *http-equiv*, *name*, *content* (required) and *scheme*.

Examples

The meta tag can be used for many different things that are dependent on the application. These are just a few things that can be done.

Refresh the Web Page

The following will refresh the page every thirty seconds.

```
<meta http-equiv="refresh" content="30"/>
```

Set the Description

The following defines the description. This is often used by search engines in the search results. Note the use of the word "often". Search engines will not use the suggested description in some cases, such as if the description doesn't appear to match the content.

```
<meta name="description" content="This is the description of the page."/>
```

Set a Revision Date

The following can be used to provide information about the freshness of the page.

```
<meta name="revised" content="Timothy Fish, 01/01/2007"/>
```

<link/>

This tag specifies the relationship between the current document and another. One common usage is to specify one or more style sheets for the document. This tag can only be used in the head of the document.

Attributes

The standard common attributes apply. Other attributes are *charset*, *href*, *hreflang*, *type*, *rel*, *rev* and *media*.

Example

The following uses the tag to link three style sheets.

```
<link rel="StyleSheet" href="style.css" type="text/css"
media="screen"/>
<link rel="StyleSheet" href="print.css" type="text/css"
media="print"/>
<link rel="StyleSheet" href="handheld.css" type="text/css"
media="handheld"/>
```

<base/>

This tag sets the base for all relative URLs on the page. This tag can only be placed in the head.

Attributes

The *href* attribute is required.

<style></style>

This tag is used to specify styles that apply to the document and none other. This tag appears only in the head. Between the tags CSS code is used.

Attributes

The *type* attribute is required. The *media* attribute also applies.

Scripting

These tags provide support for client-side scripts that are executed by the browser.

<noscript></noscript>

This tag is used to specify some text to display for browsers that do not run scripts. If the browser will run the script in a script tag then it will display nothing for this tag, but if it won't then the text between the tags will display.

<script></script>

This tag is used to mark a section of the document that is a script to be run by the browser.

Attributes

This tag has the attributes *charset, type, src, defer. Type* is required. It specifies the type of script, such as JavaScript or VBScript. The *src* attribute can be used to specify another file that contains the script rather than cluttering the XHTML file with the script. The *defer* attribute can enhance performance because it informs the browser that the script will not add content to the page and it can defer calling the script until it is no longer busy drawing the page.

Ruby Annotation

Ruby annotation is a feature of XHTML 1.1 that allows additional text to be placed above or below a base text. This can provide a pronunciation guide for words or even provide a literal translation for words written in Greek and Hebrew.

There are five tags that are used to implement Ruby Annotation. These are `ruby,` `rbc,` `rtc,` `rb,` `rt,` and `rp.`

To begin a section of Ruby text, use the <ruby></ruby> tags.

> **Example of Ruby**
>
> Hypertext Markup Language
> HTML

```
<ruby><ruby>
```

Between these put the base text using the <rb></rb> tags.
```
<ruby>
<rb>HTML</rb>
</ruby>
```

Now add the Ruby Text using <rt></rt>.
```
<ruby>
<rb>HTML</rb>
<rt>Hypertext Markup Language</rt>
</ruby>
```

This will give a result like the example.

Some browsers may not recognize Ruby, so we might want to display the result differently for them, but still use

Ruby Annotation for the others. This is possible with the
<rp></rp> (Ruby Parenthesis) tag. This tag hides what is inside if the browser knows what the tag is, otherwise the contents will be displayed. The following code will give us the results we want:

```
<ruby>
<rb>HTML</rb>
<rp>[</rp>
<rt>Hypertext Markup Language</rt>
<rp>]</rp>
</ruby>
```

Browsers that do not support Ruby will display this as:

HTML [Hypertext Markup Language]

The `rbc` and `rtc` tags can break a text into complex segments which can each have text associated with them. Consider the following code:

```
<ruby>
        <rbc>
                <rb>HT</rb>
                <rb>M</rb>
                <rb>L</rb>
        </rbc>
        <rtc>
                <rt>Hypertext</rt>
                <rt>Markup</rt>
                <rt>Language</rt>
        </rtc>
        <rtc>
                <rt rbspan="3">Ruby Text</rt>
        </rtc>
</ruby>
```

This code should produce a result that looks like the example shown here. This is a relatively new capability, so some browsers are still unable to properly display this text.

HypertextMarkupLanguage
HTML
Ruby Text

Appendix B:
Cascading Style Sheets

Cascading style sheets are used to define the intended presentation of text and other elements that are included in an XHTML page. Style sheets consist of a set of rules defined at varying levels. The first level is the browser/user settings, the next is the website settings, the next is the page settings and the last is for individual elements. In that order, each level overrides the values from the previous level.

Basic Syntax

Style sheets consist of statements or rules. The XHTML comments (<!-- -->) and white space may occur repeatedly in any order on either side of these rules. The rules look something like the following:

```
h1 { color: green; }
```

This example would cause all *h1* text to be displayed with the color green.

The more general form is:

```
selector { property: value; }
```

In the first example, *h1* is the selector, *color* is the property and *green* is the value. *Green* is a keyword that that translates into a numeric value internally.

The selector can have several things in it including the name of the element, the class and a pseudo-element giving a form that looks like:

```
Element.class:pseudo-element { property: value; }
```

Leaving off one of the three implies that all that match the others apply.

The following is the syntax to indicate a specific *id* of a matching element:

```
Element.class#element-id { property: value; }
```

Rules can also be at-rules which take on the general form:

```
@keyword parameters
```

The parameters may be a simple string or it may be several things including nested blocks.

At Rules

At rules define things related to the style sheet that is needed to process the other rules properly.

@charset

This rule specifies the character set to use. Only one charset rule is permitted. The following is an example:

```
@charset "ISO-8859-1";
```

@font-face

The font-face rule has the general form:

```
@font-face { <font-description> }
```

The <font-description> has the form:

```
descriptor: value;
descriptor: value;
[...]
```

```
descriptor: value;
```

Valid descriptors are *font-family, font-style, font-variant, font-weight, font-stretch, font-size.* A *src* can also be provided as an URL. Doing so will tell the browser where to find the font for download rather than replacing it with something that is on the user's machine.

@*import*

The import makes it possible to import styles from other style sheets. The parameter is either a string or an URL. Additional parameters are the media types. Using the additional parameters may improve performance because the browser will not need to download style sheets that it won't use.

```
@import "anotherstyle.css"
@import URL("anotherstyle.css")
@import "anotherstyle.css" print, screen
```

@*media*

The media rule specifies the media type of a set of rules so that different media types can be handled with one file.

```
@media print {
        .maintext { color: black; }
}
@media screen {
        .maintext { color: blue; }
}
```

Media types are *all, aural, Braille, embossed, handheld, print, projection, screen, tty* and *tv.*

@*page*

The page rule specifies details about the page. Page properties include *margin-top, margin-bottom, margin-right, margin-left, margin-right, margin, size* (auto, landscape, portrait or <dimensions in width height>), *marks* (crop, cross, none, inherit), *page-break-before, page-break-after, page-break-inside, page, orphans* and *widows.* Pseudo-elements are *:left* and *:right* to indicate which side of a two page layout is intended.

Pseudo-elements

Pseudo-elements serve to indicate more specific details about which elements are intended by the CSS rules.

Pseudo-element	Matches
:active	Active state of a anchor tag
:after	After the matching element
:before	Before the matching element
:first	First page of document
:first-child	First child of element
:first-letter	First letter of paragraph
:first-line	First line of paragraph
:focus	Control with focus
:hover	Link with mouse over it
:lang(L)	Element in language L
:left	Left side of two page layout
:link	Link in normal state
:right	Right side of two page layout
:visited	A visited link

CSS 2 Properties

Name	Values	Media Group
azimuth	angle+deg	aural
	left-side	
	far-left	
	left	
	center-left	
	center	
	center-right	
	right	
	far-right	
	right-side	
	behind (used with others)	
	leftwards	
	rightwards	
	inherit	
background	background-color+background-image+background-repeat+background-attachment+background-position+nn%	visual
	inherit	
background-attachment	scroll	visual
	fixed	
	inherit	
background-color	color	visual
	transparent	
	inherit	
background-image	URL("url")	visual
	none	
	inherit	

Name	Values	Media Group
background-position	nn% nn%	visual
	length+length (nn*cm, nnpx, etc.)*	
	top	
	center	
	bottom	
	left	
	center	
	right	
	top+left etc	
	inherit	
background-repeat	*repeat*	visual
	repeat-x	
	repeat-y	
	no-repeat	
	inherit	
border	border-width+border-style+color	visual
	inherit	
border-collapse	*collapse*	visual
	separate	
	inherit	
border-color	up to 4 colors	visual
	transparent	
	inherit	
border-spacing	length+length (nn*cm, nnpx, etc.)*	visual
	inherit	
border-style	up to 4 line styles	visual
	inherit	
border-top *border-right* *border-bottom* *border-left*	border-width+border-style+color	visual
	inherit	
border-top-color *border-right-color* *border-bottom-color* *border-left-color*	color	visual
	inherit	

Name	Values	Media Group
border-top-style *border-right-style* *border-bottom-style* *border-left-style*	border-style *inherit*	visual
border-top-width *border-right-width* *border-bottom-width* *border-left-width*	border-width *inherit*	visual
border-width	up to 4 border widths *inherit*	visual
bottom	length (nn*cm, nnpx, etc.*) nn% *auto* *inherit*	visual
caption-side	top *bottom* *left* *right* *inherit*	visual
clear	none *left* *right* both *inherit*	visual
clip	shape *auto* *inherit*	visual
color	color *inherit*	visual

Name	Values	Media Group
content	string	all
	URL("url")	
	counter(name)	
	counter(name, style)	
	attr(X)	
	open-quote	
	close-quote	
	no-open-quote	
	no-close-quote	
	inherit	
counter-increment	1 or more names	all
	1 or more name+step pairs	
	none	
	inherit	
counter-reset	1 or more names	all
	1 or more name+initial-value pairs	
	none	
	inherit	
cue	cue-before+cue-after	aural
	inherit	
cue-after cue-before	URL("url")	aural
	none	
	inherit	

Name	Values	Media Group
cursor	*URL("url")*	visual
	auto	interactive
	crosshair	
	default	
	pointer	
	move	
	e-resize	
	ne-resize	
	nw-resize	
	n-resize	
	se-resize	
	sw-resize	
	s-resize	
	w-resize	
	text	
	wait	
	help	
	inherit	
direction	*ltr*	visual
	rtl	
	inherit	
display	*inline*	all
	block	
	list-item	
	run-in	
	compact	
	marker	
	table	
	inline-table	
	table-row-group	
	table-header-group	
	table-footer-group	
	table-row	
	table-column-group	
	table-column	
	table-cell	
	table-caption	
	none	
	inherit	

Name	Values	Media Group
elevation	angle+*deg*	aural
	below	
	level	
	above	
	higher	
	lower	
	inherit	
empty-cells	*show*	visual
	hide	
	inherit	
float	*left*	visual
	right	
	none	
	inherit	
font	style+variant+weight+size+ line-height+family	visual
	caption	
	icon	
	menu	
	message-box	
	small-caption	
	status-bar	
	inherit	
font-family	1 or more family-name or ge-neric-family seperated by com-mas	visual
	inherit	
font-size	absolute-size	visual
	relative-size	
	length	
	nn%	
	inherit	
font-size-adjust	aspect-value	visual
	none	
	inherit	

Name	Values	Media Group
font-stretch	normal	visual
	wider	
	narrower	
	ultra-condensed	
	extra-condensed	
	condensed	
	semi-condensed	
	semi-expanded	
	expanded	
	extra-expanded	
	ultra-expanded	
	inherit	
font-style	normal	visual
	italic	
	oblique	
	inherit	
font-variant	normal	visual
	small-caps	
	inherit	
'font-weight'	normal	visual
	bold	
	bolder	
	lighter	
	100	
	200	
	300	
	400	
	500	
	600	
	700	
	800	
	900	
	inherit	
height	length	visual
	nn%	
	auto	
	inherit	

left	length	visual
	nn%	
	auto	
	inherit	
letter-spacing	normal	visual
	length	
	inherit	
line-height	normal	visual
	number	
	length	
	nn%	
	inherit	
list-style	list-style-type+ list-style-position+ list-style-image	visual
	inherit	
list-style-image	URL("url")	visual
	none	
	inherit	
list-style-position	inside	visual
	outside	
	inherit	
list-style-type	disc	visual
	circle	
	square	
	decimal	
	decimal-leading-zero	
	lower-roman	
	upper-roman	
	lower-greek	
	lower-alpha	
	lower-latin	
	upper-alpha	
	upper-latin	
	hebrew	
	armenian	
	georgian	
	cjk-ideographic	
	katakana	
	hiragana-iroha	
	katakana-iroha	
	none	
	inherit	

margin	up to 4 widths	visual
	inherit	
margin-top	margin-width	visual
margin-right	*inherit*	
margin-bottom		
margin-left		
marker-offset	length	visual
	auto	
	inherit	
marks	*crop*	visual, paged
	cross	
	crop cross	
	none	
	inherit	
max-height	length	visual
max-width	nn%	
min-height	*none*	
min-width	*inherit*	
orphans	minimum lines at bottom of page	visual, paged
	inherit	
outline	outline-color+ outline-style+ out-line-width	visual, interactive
	inherit	
outline-color	*color*	visual, interactive
	invert	
	inherit	
outline-style	border-style	visual, interactive
	inherit	
outline-width	border-width	visual, interactive
	inherit	
overflow	*visible*	visual
	hidden	
	scroll	
	auto	
	inherit	
padding	up to 4 widths	visual
	inherit	

Name	Values	Media Group
padding-top *padding-right* *padding-bottom* *padding-left*	padding-width inherit	visual
page	identifier auto	visual, paged
page-break-after *page-break-before*	auto always avoid left right inherit	visual, paged
page-break-inside	avoid auto inherit	visual, paged
pause	time time time nn% nn% nn% inherit	aural
pause-after *pause-before*	time nn% inherit	aural
pitch	frequency x-low low medium high x-high inherit	aural
pitch-range	0-100 inherit	aural
play-during	URL("url") URL("url")+*mix*+*repeat* auto none inherit	aural

Name	Values	Media Group
position	static	visual
	relative	
	absolute	
	fixed	
	inherit	
quotes	open-str+ close-str	visual
	none	
	inherit	
richness	0-100	aural
	inherit	
right	length	visual
	nn%	
	auto	
	inherit	
size	width+height	visual, paged
	auto	
	portrait	
	landscape	
	inherit	
speak	normal	aural
	none	
	spell-out	
	inherit	
speak-header	once	aural
	always	
	inherit	
speak-numeral	digits	aural
	continuous	
	inherit	
speak-punctuation	code	aural
	none	
	inherit	

Name	Values	Media Group
speech-rate	words per minute	aural
	x-slow	
	slow	
	medium	
	fast	
	x-fast	
	faster	
	slower	
	inherit	
stress	0-100	aural
	inherit	
table-layout	*auto*	visual
	fixed	
	inherit	
text-align	*left*	visual
	right	
	center	
	justify	
	matching string	
	inherit	
text-decoration	*none*	visual
	underline+ overline+ line-through+ blink	
	inherit	
text-indent	length	visual
	nn%	
	inherit	
text-shadow	*none*	visual
	comma seperated list of color+length+length+length	
	inherit	
text-transform	*capitalize*	visual
	uppercase	
	lowercase	
	none	
	inherit	
top	length	visual
	nn%	
	auto	
	inherit	

Name	Values	Media Group
unicode-bidi	*normal*	visual
	embed	
	bidi-override	
	inherit	
vertical-align	*baseline*	visual
	sub	
	super	
	top	
	text-top	
	middle	
	bottom	
	text-bottom	
	nn%	
	length	
	inherit	
visibility	*visible*	visual
	hidden	
	collapse	
	inherit	
voice-family	comma seperated list of specific or generic voices	aural
	inherit	
volume	*0-100*	aural
	nn%	
	silent (not same as 0)	
	x-soft (same as 0)	
	soft	
	medium	
	loud	
	x-loud (same as 100)	
	inherit	
white-space	*normal*	visual
	pre	
	nowrap	
	inherit	
widows	minimum lines at top of page	visual, paged
	inherit	

Name	Values	Media Group
width	length	visual
	nn%	
	auto	
	inherit	
word-spacing	normal	visual
	length	
	inherit	
z-index	auto	visual
	integer	
	inherit	

This know also, that in the last days perilous times shall come.

–   II Timothy 3:1